SIMPLE FENG SHUI

S I M P L E

FENG SHUI

Damian Sharp

CASTLE BOOKS

This edition published in 2002 by Castle Books,
A division of Book Sales Inc.
114 Northfield Avenue, Edison, NJ 08837

Published by arrangement with Conari Press, 2550 Ninth Street, Suite 101,
Berkeley, CA 94710-2551.

Cover and book design: Claudia Smelser
Cover illustration: Suzanne Albertson
Interior illustrations: Lei Yang

   LIBRARY OF CONGRESS CATALOGING-IN-PUBLICATION DATA
Sharp, Damian
   Simple feng shui / Damian Sharp.
         p.   cm.
Included bibliographical references and index.
   1. Feng-shui I. Title II. Series
BF1779.F4S475   1999
133.3'337—dc21   99-21083
                                                               CIP

Printed in the United States of America.

ISBN: 0-7858-1510-4

To Lei Yang

SIMPLE FENG SHUI

one The Fascinating Art and Science of Feng Shui   1

two The Positive and Negative Influence
of Nature on Our Buildings   15

three Creating Good Feng Shui
Inside Your Home or Office   63

four Determining the Best Use for Each Room   77

To Learn More   97

Index   101

one

THE FASCINATING ART
AND SCIENCE OF FENG SHUI

Observe the mountains and rivers to know the yin and the yang,
Observe the streams and springs to know the source of the waters.

—From the *Shih-ching*
(*Book of Poetry*, c. 800–600 B.C.)

In recent years, Westerners have become very interested in}
Feng Shui, the ancient Taoist art and science of living in harmony with the environment. Feng Shui is a way of understand-
ing the flow of the Earth's energy and cooperating with it rather
than opposing it, and of channeling it for beneficial results.

The ancient Chinese observed how the erratic influences of
wind and water could be affected by alterations in the contours
and shapes of the landscape. They saw, for instance, how the
building of high towers could result in gusting winds, how the
digging of wells could cause natural streams to dry up, and how
diverting waters for irrigation could leach the soil, causing salts
to rise up and make once-fertile land arid. If these human

changes could affect such powerful natural forces, it was only logical that they would exert equally as profound an influence on the lives and affairs of human beings. These ancients also came to believe that each building has its own "life," determined by its location, orientation, design, surroundings, and even the time it was built, some being blessed by good fortune and others cursed by misfortune. From these perceptions came a whole system of observing, enhancing, and altering the flow of natural energies.

Feng Shui offers us a different way of seeing the world, and when practiced, its effect on the way we view things around us is profound indeed. That's because Feng Shui makes us aware that energy resides in all things, and that the way energy flows or doesn't flow has a significant effect on our happiness and well-being.

For centuries Feng Shui has been used by the Chinese to select building sites, design homes, cities, and towns, and bury the dead. There are two kinds of Feng Shui: *Yang,* which deals with the orientation and shape of buildings and objects, and *Yin,* which deals with graves and tombs. There are many Chinese stories and legends about ghosts, unhappy with their graves because of the bad Feng Shui of a burial site, who return to haunt the living.

This book is a simple and very basic introduction to Yang Feng Shui and is designed to help you make changes to your en-

vironment that will enhance the positive effects of your surroundings and counter those that are harmful.

Yin and yang are the two complementary polarities of Taoist
philosophy. Taoism is one of the three major religions of ancient China (the other two are Confucianism and Buddhism);
tradition holds that it was founded around the sixth century
B.C. by Lao-tzu. The term *Tao* means "the Way," or the forces
inherent in nature; it also refers to a code of behavior that is in
harmony with the natural order, as set down in the *Tao-te-
Ching,* Taoism's most sacred scripture, which was written by
Lao-tzu. The goal of Taoism is, through self-discipline and un-
derstanding, to become one with the Tao itself, to be in complete harmony with the invisible and visible forces of nature.

According to Taoism, first there was spirit, or Heaven, which
the Taoists represented as a circle. After Heaven, there was matter, or Earth, which they represented as a square within the circle.
From Heaven and Earth, the Taoists developed the philosophy of
yin and yang. Yin is female, negative, dark, soft, still, the recep-
tive, the Earth. Yang is male, positive, light, hard, dynamic, the
creative, Heaven. Light and dark are the two primal powers, also
known as firm and yielding, and as day and night.

In Taoism, light (yang) and dark (yin) designate the two primal powers of nature. These terms are extended to include the
two polar forces of the universe: the positive and the negative. It
is the Tao (the Way) that sets these two opposites in motion and

T'ai chi t'u, the circular
Taoist symbol of yin and yang

maintains the interplay of the two forces.
These two designations, light and dark, which
symbolize and emphasize the cycle of change,
led to the representation of the familiar symbol of yin and yang,
T'ai chi t'u—the Primal Beginning—which is the keystone of
Taoist thought.

The two opposite principles of yin and yang complement
rather than compete with each other. Neither one dominates or
defeats the other. Both are needed to complete and balance the
universe. To illustrate this, in the *T'ai chi t'u,* a small white spot
is included within the yin (dark) and a small black spot in the
yang (light).

Chi, the universal life energy, flows between spirit and matter.
Chi is neither yin nor yang, but enhances both, always flowing
between the two, seeking a natural balance. When the flow of
chi is unencumbered, our lives are enriched; when it is disrupted
or distorted, it turns into a negative form of energy known as
sha, which can cause sickness, conflict, loss, destruction, and
even death. *Chi,* like wind and water, moves in gentle, flowing
curves (represented by the S-curve in the *T'ai chi t'u*) and retains
a temporary impression of whatever it has flowed around. *Sha,*
on the other hand, moves in hard straight lines.

The viewpoint of Feng Shui is not unique to the Chinese; elements of it can be found in the religious beliefs of nearly all indigenous peoples, from Australian Aborigines to the people of Bali and Indonesia to the native tribes of Southeast Asia and the Pacific, the Americas, Siberia, and Africa. In Europe, the awe-inspiring sense of the innate and hidden powers in nature was central to the beliefs of the ancient Greeks, the Celts, and the Romans. All share a common sense of awe and reverence for the natural world, and all have rules concerning human behavior in relation to the absolute respect for nature. The remarkable thing about Feng Shui is that it represents a sensibility shared with all of these cultures, and is the product of a highly advanced and complex civilization.

When we practice Feng Shui, we are acting as responsible stewards and guardians of the environment and ensuring a continued and pragmatic reverence for and preservation of the natural beauty and innate life-giving spirit-force of our planet—the Earth.

In the late twentieth century, Feng Shui is finding increasing acceptance in the West among architects, city planners, landscape and interior designers, real estate agents, business executives, and homeowners. In Hong Kong, Taiwan, Singapore, and other places where there are large Chinese populations, it is regularly employed as a matter-of-fact and vital part of everyday life.

The practice of Feng Shui requires the maximum use of your visual imagination along with an informed and heightened intuition, a way of seeing the land as alive and its forms vital and sentient, filled with a language that quietly informs you. This may be magic, instinct, and even science; it may be something else yet that incorporates these three elements and is called Feng Shui.

SHAMANIC ORIGINS

The principles of Feng Shui are derived from the Chinese classics that were written thousands of years ago and are Taoist in origin, primarily the *I Ching,* or Book of Changes, which has been used in China for divination for centuries and is considered a sacred text; and the *Li Shu,* or Book of Rites, a sacred text that outlined the tenets of Chinese religious beliefs, and even dictated which rooms of the palace the Emperor should occupy according to the season, month, and year.

The Chinese characters *Feng* and *Shui* literally mean "wind" and "water," which gives us a valuable hint about the origins of Feng Shui as a divinational art that was practiced by the tribal shaman-kings of ancient China. The Feng Shui masters of China's dynastic period were regarded as the successors of the *fang-shih* tradition of Taoism. The *fang-shih,* or masters, were magicians, diviners, doctors, and internal alchemists of the first and second centuries. Feng Shui is consequently closely related to the other Taoist arts.

According to legend, the shaman-kings knew the ways of

wind and water, understood the underlying nature of landforms and their effects on weather, and possessed power over the elements, by which means they led and protected their people. One such legendary shaman-king was Fu Hsi, who is recognized as the patron of all the divinational arts of China. It is said that up until his birth humans lived like beasts, clad in animal skins and eating raw flesh. He taught the people to hew wood, hunt, fish, cook, and make musical instruments. He is, we might say, the legendary bringer of civilization to the Chinese people. Fu Hsi was knowledgeable in the ways of animals, and in paintings he is often depicted wearing a tiger skin and accompanied by a tortoise and a snake.

There are many differing accounts of the legend of Fu Hsi, but from what we can discern, he was the first of the Chinese emperors in legendary times, and is credited with the invention of the *Lo Shu,* said to have been revealed to him on the back of a magical tortoise, and the Eight Trigrams of the *I Ching.* The *Lo Shu*—Book or Writing of the River Lo—is a mystic diagram that is in fact the mathematical "magic square" arrangement of the numbers one to nine so that they add up to fifteen in all directions. The Eight Trigrams, known as the *pa-k'ua* (which also represent the eight directions of the Taoist compass), are each made up of a series of combinations of three broken and unbroken lines, and are the earliest known example of binary notation. You will often see them placed on the sides of an octagon, a popular Chinese talisman for warding off evil.

The *Lo Shu* appearing on the back of a tortoise

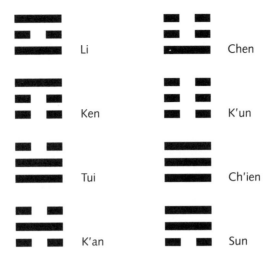

Li   Chen

Ken   K'un

Tui   Ch'ien

K'an   Sun

The *pa-k'ua,* the Eight Trigrams of the *I Ching*

Another great shaman-king was Huang-Ti, who became the Yellow Emperor. Having lost his way while fighting a bandit chieftain whose magical powers had caused fog to envelop the mountain valleys, Huang-Ti was given by the Lady of the Nine Heavens a compass that enabled him to outwit and capture his enemy. During his reign the stems and branches for reckoning time were instituted, astronomical instruments constructed, a calendar compiled, mathematical studies pursued, garments tailored, and objects of wood, metal, and pottery manufactured.

The Chinese character *Huang* means "Sovereign." The first emperor of a united China combined *Huang* and *Ti* ("Emperor") to call himself Huang-Ti, the First Sovereign Emperor (a title not used again until the reign of the Manchus beginning in the seventeenth century). *Huang,* written in a different character, also means "yellow," and before the Chinese empire had amalgamated several different states, the Chinese or Han nation occupied an area on a bend in the Yellow River, regarded as the center of China. China was and is called the Middle Kingdom; the color yellow *(huang),* which was associated with the Middle Kingdom, not only represents China and "imperial" power but the Earth as well. Pu Yi, the last emperor of China, wrote that as a boy he believed everything to be yellow because he saw so much of the color.

Yet another among these legendary greats was Yü, also known as Yü the Great, said to be a descendant of Huang Ti. According to legend, Yü was an ugly cripple. His father having failed to drain the floodwaters, Yü was appointed to the task (purportedly in 2286 B.C.), and after nine years accomplished his mission, as well as a survey of the country, which he divided into nine provinces. In 2224 B.C. the Emperor Shun raised him to the position of Regent. After Shun's death he ascended the throne. His most spectacular achievement was a canal known as Yü's Tunnel, one of the great wonders of the Chinese landscape, which featured three successive cuttings stretching for over two hundred miles through the Wu Shan Mountains in

Szechuan. In legend, Yü is often associated with Fu Hsi, whom he is said to have met while excavating the channel to drain the floods. The sage, by this time an Immortal with a human face and a serpent's body, is said to have given Yü a jade instrument for measuring Heaven and Earth. It is sometimes said that the *Lo Shu* was given to Yü, a confusion possibly arising from his division of the country into nine provinces (the *pa-k'ua* is composed of the eight directions plus the center; the *Lo Shu* the numbers one to nine). Yü founded the Hsia Dynasty, long believed to have been a mythical era, but archaeological evidence now reveals that classical references to the Hsia are not invention, but indeed are based on fact. The Hsia Dynasty ruled for over four hundred years before being overthrown by the Shang. One version of the *I Ching,* the Book of Changes, known as the *Lin-shan-i,* is attributed to Yü.

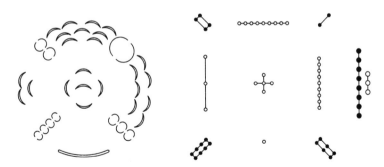

Ancient and modern renditions of *Lo-shu*

After six hundred years, the Shang Dynasty was in its turn overthrown by the Duke of Chou, who became known as King Wen, founder of the Chou Dynasty. Wen, adept at divination and possessing a deep comprehension of the cyclical nature of the universe, used the *Lo-shu* to predict the course of historical events and expanded the Eight Trigrams of the *pa-k'ua* into the sixty-four hexagrams of the *Chou-i,* fragments of which were later compiled by Confucius into the *I Ching* that we know today. King Wen rightly predicted his own capture and imprisonment, his son's death, and his eventual defeat of his enemy.

THE FIRST BOOKS ON FENG SHUI

In the ninth century A.D., the scholar Yang Yun-sung, living amid the awesomely beautiful and strangely shaped hills and mountains surrounding Kuelin in southern China, wrote the first book on Feng Shui, describing and systematizing the various characteristics and attributes of land formations. This text was to become the standard manual of the "Form School" of Feng Shui. A century later, in the plains of northern China, a second book was written, this one outlining a means of analyzing the Feng Shui of mountainless regions and laying out the precepts for a second school of Feng Shui known as the "Compass School." Today, Feng Shui practitioners combine these two systems, looking first at the shapes of the surrounding landscape and then consulting a geomantic compass (the *lo-p'an*) to note the alignments of mountains and rivers in proximity to the site under consideration and its position in relation to the eight cardinal points or directions (represented by the *pa-k'ua*, or Eight Trigrams of the *I Ching*).

two

THE POSITIVE AND NEGATIVE INFLUENCE OF NATURE ON OUR BUILDINGS

We begin from the outside, looking at the elements in nature, because Feng Shui is properly done from the perspective of the external environment first. It's important to understand the effects of the energy flow from the external environment of your home or office, so you can use this knowledge when choosing a place to live or work, and to understand what remedies you might need to adopt if you are in an unfavorable location.

Feng Shui, first and foremost, assesses a location's environment to determine whether the external conditions are beneficial or adverse, how adverse conditions can be countered, and how beneficial influences can be maximized. Environmental features can be both natural and constructed, with natural features taking precedence over artificial.

In Feng Shui, all land can be described as mountain and water, or yin and yang. Generally speaking, mountains are yin and still, while water is yang and dynamic. In places where there are only mountains and no water, the flow of energy is diminished. If there is water but no mountains, the energy will be difficult to harness. Remember that terrestrial harmony occurs in the *balance* of yin and yang. For a place to have power, its energy must not be static, nor must it be scattered. Hence the best Feng Shui sites, and the best places to live, are those that have both mountains and water.

According to certain theorists, the Great Wall of China was built not only to keep out northern nomadic invaders like the Manchurians, Huns, other tribes such as the Khitans, Uighurs, Tatars, and Merkits, and steppe tribes who would become known as the Mongols, but also as a Feng Shui conduit of the Earth's energy. Mist wafting over a verdant mountainside (a common theme in classical Chinese painting) is said to indicate the copulation of sky and earth energies (yang and yin). Such locations are filled with power, as *chi,* creative energy, is born from this interaction. Canyons surrounded by steep cliffs, on the other hand, are considered unfavorable sites for building houses, as such locations tend to be wind tunnels that carry negative or destructive energy (*sha*). Also, houses should not be built facing or overlooking a road cutting that exposes harsh layers of rocks—harsh-looking rocks are another conveyor of *sha,* as are fast-flowing water and water that crashes violently onto land. Therefore it is considered harmful to live in a house atop a sea cliff or on the banks of a fast-flowing stream. Water that laps gently as it meets the land is beneficial, and a house looking out onto a beach and trees is highly desirable, as is a house that has a view of the sea in which differences in coloration and surface patterns (known as Dragon formations, which bring nourishing energy) can be discerned.

Artificially created landforms and buildings are called Later Heaven Formations and do not have inherent energy when compared with natural landforms. Natural landforms are called Earlier Heaven Formations; because they have been created over the millennia and have absorbed the energy of the universe, they are considered superior to artificial forms. Artificial formations can, however, direct the flow of energy or act as protectors from harmful or destructive energy. Large-scale artificial formations include dams, canals, and reservoirs. Small-scale artificial formations include walls, hedges, ponds, fountains, and gardens. Ancient structures like the Pyramids, the Great Wall, Stonehenge, and other megalithic constructions, however, may contain energy, as they have been in existence long enough to have absorbed it from the environment. Time or age, then, can be a crucial factor in assessing energy. This applies to recently made natural formations as well, such as volcanoes, which owing to their geological youth have not been around long enough to gather energy. Such formations, though, may conduct or block the flow of energy.

When a natural landform that harbors energy is destroyed, the power contained in the land is destroyed along with it. Cutting a roadway or tunneling through a mountain, flooding a valley, draining a swamp, and reclaiming land from the sea are common examples of the destruction of both the natural landforms and the energy that is contained within them.

The energy embodied in a landform can also be altered by the structures that are built upon it. The imposition of sharp points and angles on a rounded mountaintop (for example, erecting transmitters and antennas) will often turn benevolent and positive energy into energy that is negative and harmful.

The earliest writers on Feng Shui claimed that the south-facing side of a hill represented the best location for building, with a stream flowing along one side of the structure, turning in front of the site, and then disappearing underground. This, on the surface, seems to be nothing more than common sense. The south side of a slope receives the most sunlight, the hill at the back provides protection from north winds, and the stream is a convenient and necessary source of water. But although Feng Shui is based on sound scientific principles, there is definitely more to it than mere common sense.

THE DRAGON AND THE TIGER, THE RAVEN AND THE TORTOISE

According to Feng Shui, the more a hill or skyline resembles a dragon, the greater the energetic efficacy of the site in question. The Feng Shui practitioner, when first examining a location, looks for the dragon apparent in the landscape, discerning its limbs, head, body, and tail. A raised head is considered very for-

tunate, and if there is a stream or pool of water near the
dragon's mouth—the classical Chinese motif called "dragon
salivating pearls"—then the influence is at its most auspicious,
ensuring wealth and success for whoever builds there. It is,
however, extremely dangerous to build on, cut across, or in any
way alter those features deemed to be parts of the dragon's
body. Trees that define its form must not be cut down, and to
slice across the dragon's veins—thus killing the dragon—is to
invite disaster.

In Feng Shui, animals from Chinese astronomy are used to
represent the four directions as well as the front, right, left, and
back sides of a building. The four celestial animals are also associated with the four points of the compass and the four seasons, as shown in the following table.

Animal	Season	Direction	Side of Building
Dragon	Spring	East	Left
Raven	Summer	South	Front
Tiger	Autumn	West	Right
Tortoise	Winter	North	Back

Thus, when the front of a site faces south, the four Feng Shui
terms correspond directly to the directions of the compass. But
the two sets of terms are not always interchangeable. When applied to a building, the Raven is always at the entrance, even if
it isn't facing south, the Tortoise is at the back, the Dragon is to
the left, and the Tiger is to the right.

An "ideal" south-facing site

A west-facing site   A north-facing site

In assessing the overall Feng Shui of a locality, the four animal names are applied to the four points of the compass, with each animal also having its own color, thus:

Direction	Color	Animal
North	Black	Tortoise
South	Red	Raven
East	Green	Dragon
West	White	Tiger

Different types of *chi* flow from each of the different directions; each of the animals represents the way the *chi* flows. From the north (the realm of the Black Tortoise), the *chi* is listless; from the south (the Red Raven), it is energetic; from the west (the White Tiger), erratic and unpredictable; and from the east (the Green Dragon), nurturing and protective.

FACING WALLS

Internal and external walls are named according to the direction they face. The entrance to a building, and the interior wall facing it, are represented by the Raven. The exterior of that same wall, though, is represented by the Tortoise. Similarly, the external left wall is represented by the Dragon, as is the internal side of the opposite wall (the Tiger), as that side, too, is facing left. The internal side of the external Dragon wall is represented by the Tiger, as that side of the wall faces right.

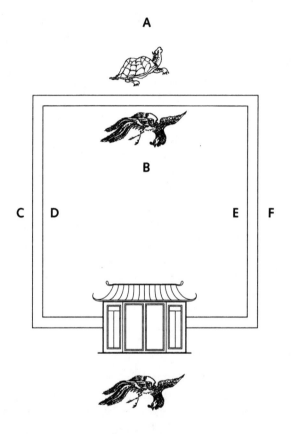

Interior and exterior walls represented by animals from Chinese astrology

The very best of all possible sites for buildings are those where the four animal symbols—Dragon, Raven, Tiger, and Tortoise—are easily discernible in the landforms surrounding the location in question. These symbolic landforms—or animals—are the guardians of the place. Depending on their formations, some guardians will be more effective than others. As well as the four cardinal points, the Green Dragon, White Tiger, Red Raven, and Black Tortoise are named after the four animal protector spirits that were identified by the ancient Chinese shamans. They are all harbingers of protective energy. If all four are not present, three is considered to be very fortunate; and if not three, then the Dragon alone, or the Tiger, will serve to establish the presence of the four symbolic creatures. Above all, the Dragon should be visible, and identifying the Dragon's presence is the first priority of the Feng Shui expert in evaluating the Feng Shui of a site.

The Dragon's vein is a path of concentrated Earth energy that is characteristic of mountain landscapes. It is believed to emanate the "breath of the Dragon," the invisible force that gives life to the Earth. Mountains with Dragon veins contain magnetic fields, many of which follow a magnetic direction. In Feng Shui, walking along these paths is called "chasing the Dragon."

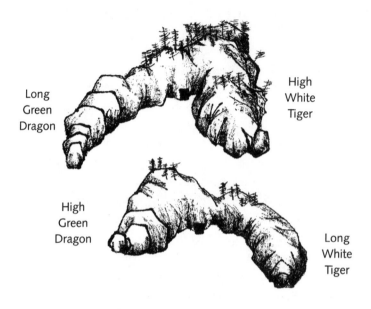

Long
Green
Dragon

High
White
Tiger

High
Green
Dragon

Long
White
Tiger

Examples of landforms showing the Dragon and the Tiger

Dragon veins are classified as kingly or ordinary, coherent or scattered. They can be strong or weak, nourishing or destructive, depending on their pattern. An example of a Dragon vein can be seen in the branches of a mountain range coming together and continuing like the spine of a dragon. A vein may also begin where there are a few solitary peaks with steep slopes. A strong vein is organized, follows a straight path, and has many branches. A weak vein twists around, and its branches are sparse and disconnected. An energizing vein has a large trunk and thick branches. In a destructive vein, the branches are disconnected and end in a cliff, or there is a branch that cuts into the main trunk. A dead vein has no branches at all. Veins in mountain ranges that have many branches with numerous peaks, ridges, and valleys are called kingly. Veins in smaller ranges are ordinary. Coherent veins follow a continuous path and form an organized pattern. Scattered veins are discontinuous and random. When a vein ends abruptly in a peak or steep slope it is called "the sudden death" of the Dragon vein, and indicates a location that is extremely harmful. A place is said to swallow the life-giving energy of the Dragon when a vein terminates gently into it. The more veins that terminate into a location, the more energy that location absorbs, and the more powerful and life-enhancing it is.

The Dragon and the Tiger are an inseparable polarity and always coexist, like north and south and yin and yang. If the Dragon is present, then by default so is the Tiger, even though the Tiger may be hidden.

The ideal Feng Shui site is situated between two hills, one to the east, the other to the west. The eastern hill, the Dragon, should always be the higher of the two, and preferably covered with grass or a stand of trees. It should not be rocky or sandy or cut into by gullies. An effective White Tiger should be a strong rock formation with no sharp features. When the slope of one

The Dragon and Tiger in an embrace

hill flows out from behind that of the other, the line of their
escarpments overlapping, it is considered to be most beneficial,
a representation of the Dragon and the Tiger in an embrace.
When the Dragon and the Tiger appear in a geographic formation that resemble arms cradling the site, then the site is deemed
both protected and extremely auspicious. The more layers of
arms, of course, the better the protection from maleficent
forces.

To the north there should be distant and higher hills, or a
stand of conifers, which represent the Black Tortoise. The south
should be open, and, ideally, facing a gentle slope or depression,
with a distant rock or some other form readily identifiable as
the Red Raven. The Red Raven should not be a dominant feature that might overshadow the building; this would mean bad
Feng Shui.

In an urban environment, an effective Green Dragon is ideally a building with a greenish or bluish tint. Buildings with
trees or hedges on their sides or with ivy clinging to their walls
are also acceptable as Dragons. The White Tiger should be a
building with a white stone facade, or a building that is simply
painted white. The building should be squat and strong. If the
Green Dragon building is tall, then the White Tiger should be
long, and vice versa. The Red Raven in front should be a building that is lower than the site, preferably long, and not too
close. The Black Tortoise buildings at the back should be higher
than the site and again not too close.

Chi is a much-used term in Chinese, meaning "breath," "air," "energy," and even "life-force." We see its use in such terms as *T'ai Chi* and *Chi Gong.* In Feng Shui, it can equally be applied to healthy currents of air as well as the invisible energies flowing through a room or house. Positive currents of *chi,* particularly those generated by a Dragon hill (from which they emanate in abundance), are said to produce a healthy and harmonious environment, prolong life, and even bring material prosperity.

According to Feng Shui, *chi* should be able to enter the site or building at one end, flow around it, and leave through the opposite side. A room with, say, only one door and no windows lacks the means by which the *chi* is able to circulate, thus the *chi* dies and becomes stagnant. Such places should only be used for storage. In rooms that require a more vibrant atmosphere, such as living rooms and work spaces, *chi* can be enhanced or excited by the use of mirrors that reflect the *chi* back and forth. Places of rest, study, or meditation should be designed in such a way that the *chi* is gently channeled through; if the bedroom is considered not so much a place of sleep as an arena of excited activity, then, like the work place or living room, mirrors can be strategically employed. According to some Feng Shui theorists, though, it is not good to have a mirror in your bedroom, as it is believed that the soul rises from the body during sleep and may become startled by the sight of its own reflection. Having a mirror in your bedroom, then, is a matter of personal belief and discretion.

SOURCES OF *SHA*

The opposite of *chi* is *sha*, the negative energies or currents that have adverse effects on the people residing in a location that is subject to the *sha* influence. While beneficial *chi* permeates an environment by gently meandering through it, *sha* travels in hard straight lines. An example of this belief can be seen in certain old bridges in China that lead across streams directly to the doors of pagodas and dwellings—the bridges are built in a zigzag pattern to prevent harmful *sha* and evil spirits from crossing. It is the Feng Shui master's task to analyze how the beneficial *chi* can be harnessed to permeate the site and the baleful *sha* adequately deflected.

Sha is produced by geographical faults and fissures in the earth. Natural gullies directed in a straight line toward the site are also sources of *sha*, as they are, in non-esoteric terms, a direct source of danger in times of exceptional rainfall and flood.

Buildings with corners that are at an angle pointing directly at the site are a source of a particular kind of *sha* called "a secret arrow." The angled corner is like a bow, drawn with an arrow aimed directly at the site, and is a conduit of harmful energy. People living in the target area are likely to suffer from chronic illnesses and any variety of continual misfortune, because their energy is depleted.

Roads that lead directly up to a house and then turn at a sharp right angle are especially harmful, as they combine the bad effects of ordinary *sha* with "the secret arrow." Tunnels or railways that approach the site are also conveyors of *sha*.

A house that has its back door directly opposite and visible from the front door, or is divided by a central passageway, is regarded as having bad Feng Shui. A house designed in this manner is, literally, a house divided against itself. Opposition and conflict are bound to occur within its walls. The central passageway not only channels negative *sha* but also acts to scatter and disperse the positive *chi*. A room that has windows opposite each other has no fixed point around which the *chi* is able to flow. Instead, the *chi* passes right through it without being able to exert any beneficial influence. For the same reason, stairs should not be directly opposite the front door, and should turn about halfway up.

Power cables and telephone wires are also conductors of *sha* and should approach a building at an oblique angle. Telephone poles, lamp posts, and tall trees should never be positioned before a front window. They represent the conifers of the north and are inappropriate for the Red Raven side of the building. The straight shadows cast by columns and poles are also sources of malevolent *sha*.

Taoism recognizes five elements (not four as in the West). These are Metal, Wood, Water, Earth, and Fire; they correspond to the four cardinal directions as well as to the center of the *pa-k'ua*, the arrangement of the Eight Trigrams. As we have already seen, each of the four directions represents a season—east: spring; south: summer; west: autumn; and north: winter—a color, and an element. The center represents only a color and an element.

Direction	Season	Color	Element
East	Spring	Green	Wood
South	Summer	Red	Fire
Center		Yellow	Earth
West	Autumn	White	Metal
North	Winter	Black	Water

This is the principle order of the elements, from which each element generates or begets the next: Wood burns, creating Fire, which produces ash, or Earth, from which is obtained Metal, which, when melted, liquefies like Water, which then nourishes the Earth, out of which grows Wood, and so on.

Elements that are next to each are considered to help one another: Wood helps Fire, Water helps Wood. This is called the "Generative Order." When two elements stand opposite each other in this series, one destroys the other. Wood destroys Earth; Earth destroys Water; Water destroys Fire; Fire destroys Metal; Metal destroys Wood. This is called the "Destructive Order" of the elements.

When assessing the Feng Shui of a site, you must first determine the predominant elements surrounding it. From these you can then determine the governing element of the site itself. This is extremely important; you must ensure that the site and its location are in harmony. The most obvious way by which a location reveals its elemental qualities is by its *shape*. One of the fascinating things about Feng Shui is that these elements are not considered literally; that is, the elemental factors are not determined by whether wood, fire, earth, metal, or water are actually present at a site, but whether the shape of the land formations *suggests* the elements.

Wood: The Wood element is suggested by tall soaring hills with flat tops that slope gently down, and by structures such as towers, poles, pillars, chimneys, and tall narrow skyscrapers.

Fire: The Fire element is seen in triangular-shaped mountains with sharp, pointed peaks, church spires, and other steeply roofed buildings, such as pagodas.

Earth: The Earth element is suggested by flatness and is seen in plateaus, tables, or flat-top mountains whose slopes drop suddenly and steeply, and flat-roofed buildings.

Metal: The Metal element is found in mountains with rounded summits and gentle slopes and in buildings with domed roofs.

Water: The Water element is characterized by undulating hills, mountains with uneven slopes and round tops, the actual presence of water, and by buildings of complex and predominantly rounded design.

THE SYMBOLIC MEANING OF THE FIVE ELEMENTS

Feng Shui also considers the symbolic meaning of each element.

Wood, representing spring, the seasonal beginning of the new year, is symbolic of creation, nourishment, and growth. Its shape is tall and upright (as in a tree). Restaurants, hospitals,

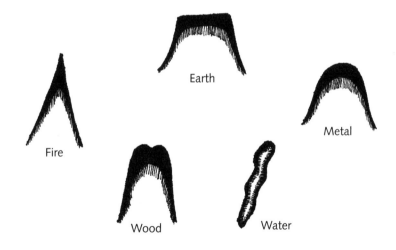

The five elemental shapes

nurseries, residences, and commercial establishments concerned with creativity (such as an advertising agency) all benefit from the influence of the Wood element.

Fire is said to represent intellect, and Fire-shaped buildings are therefore most appropriate for libraries and all institutions of learning. Fire's color, red, is also associated with blood, livestock, and, along with Metal, butchery. Manufacturing based on fire and furnaces, plastics, and chemical processing also belong to the Fire element.

Earth is, naturally, found in any buildings made of brick, clay, or concrete, no matter what the shape. A brick house with a pointed sloping roof belongs to both the Earth and Fire elements, a good combination since Fire and Earth belong to the Generative Order of the elements. Blocks of flats and offices and low flat-topped buildings have the Earth shape and belong to this element. Earth-type buildings are solid, stable, and durable, but lack any stimulating attributes. They are considered "immobile" and therefore best suited as places of storage, such as warehouses or, as in the case of the Earth area of a house, a garage or basement. Industries such as farming, building, mining, ceramics production, and civil engineering belong to the Earth element.

Metal buildings are characterized by domes and curved roofs and arches. Metal is symbolic of money; these structural shapes are ideal for banks and other financial institutions, which, inter-

estingly enough, often favor them. A combination of Earth and
Metal elements in a building is considered to be extremely fortuitous, as these two elements stand together in the Generative
Order and guarantee financial success and wealth. Any manufacturing or commerce involved with metal obviously falls
under this category. The Metal element, however, is not suitable
for domestic life. In the home, any area under the auspices of
this element should be used exclusively as a work place.

Water is seen in buildings of irregular design and construction, and in buildings in which there is a predominance of glass.
A Water building will often appear to have the mixed characteristics of all four other elements. Water is the element of commu-
nication, and all businesses and institutions concerned with the
transmission of ideas and information will benefit from its influence. Naturally, industries involving liquid, such as brewing and
distilling, also fall into this category.

INFLUENCES OF THE FIVE ELEMENTS

A site may be classified as belonging to two or more elements,
known as a "compound site" or building. The following are the
Feng Shui auguries or forecasts for the five basic sites within the
five types of location or environment. You can use this list to
determine if your house, apartment, or office building is appro-
priately situated for the best Feng Shui.

Naturally, this is a structure either made of wood or categorized as belonging to the Wood shape, such as a tower-like building.

Wood Environment/Wood Site

The Wood environment is often characterized by surrounding woods and forests, neighboring buildings made of wood, or the presence of columns and posts that are part of some larger construction, such as a bridge. A wooden structure in a Wood environment is stable. If the environment is defined by other Wood structures, it is desirable for the function of the building to match those surrounding it. If the environmental element is determined from the features of the landscape (such as trees or tall columnar rocks), then the site is suitable for all forms of creative activity, nourishment, care, and agriculture.

Fire Environment/Wood Site

The Fire environment is seen in buildings with steep roofs or sharp angles and, in the countryside, in distant mountain peaks. As Wood fuels Fire, this site is likely to give more to its surroundings than it will receive. The proposed building would be best used as something that gives to the community, like a school, church, or hospital. With this combination, commercial success is not assured, and homes are faced with the possibility of destruction by fire.

Earth Environment/Wood Site

The Earth environment is depicted in flat plains, flat-topped mountains, and by low, flat-roofed buildings. Wood destroys Earth by taking nourishment from it. Here, the site takes, rather than gives, to its surroundings, a situation that can bring substantial benefits to the dwelling's occupants, but only for the short term, as the positive influences are quickly depleted.

Metal Environment/Wood Site

The Metal environment is characterized by rounded hills and by buildings with domes or arches. Since Metal destroys Wood, this combination harbors potential danger to those working or dwelling within it. Nor does it bode well for the success of any commercial enterprise.

Water Environment/Wood Site

A Water environment is one in which water is actually present—lakes, rivers, streams, and ponds—and is also characterized by low undulating hills and in buildings that have irregular shapes. As Water feeds Wood, this is a very beneficial combination in which the success of all business enterprises, as well as the well-being and happiness of those inhabiting the dwelling, is assured.

——— The Fire Site ———

Fire is the element of animal life, chemical change, and human intelligence. The only building materials that fall into its category are those derived from animals, like skins or synthetic fabrics. In terms of materials, then, Fire-type structures tend to be limited to tents. In terms of shape, as we have already seen, Fire-type buildings are characterized by steep-sloped roofs and sharp, angular contours.

Wood Environment/Fire Site

Wood feeds Fire. A Wood environment nourishes a Fire site, making this combination beneficial for both business enterprises and residential dwellings. The Chinese believe that children born and raised under the auspices of this combination of environment and site will be very intelligent. Also, the site is particularly well suited to the rearing of livestock, industries that deal with chemical processing, and institutions of learning.

Fire Environment/Fire Site

This is considered to be beneficial although highly volatile. Only short-term or transient businesses and dwellings are recommended. These may thrive gloriously for a while, but will then become spent, according to the nature of the double-Fire combination. "Its coming is sudden; It flames up, dies down, is thrown away" (from the *I Ching*).

Earth Environment/Fire Site

Earth represents the ash made by Fire. Those living in a Fire house in an Earth environment will be content with their lot and enjoy the goodwill, gratitude, and respect of their neighbors. Although businesses will not prosper as in some other combinations, they will reap the benefits of having a reputation for honesty and integrity.

Metal Environment/Fire Site

Fire melts Metal. This combination favors any enterprise bent on ruthlessly reaping a profit from its surroundings. For those who inhabit it, it promises social and political success.

Water Environment/Fire Site

Water extinguishes Fire. This is, cut and dried, a bad combination.

The Earth Site

The Earth element is, as we have said earlier, seen in buildings that are flat and square and also in constructions made from earthen materials such as brick and concrete. It is, however, principally form and not material that determines a site's element.

Wood Environment/Earth Site

Wood conquers Earth. Wood destroys Earth by taking nourishment from it. Here, the site takes, rather than gives, to its surroundings, a situation that can bring substantial benefits to the dwelling's occupants, but only for the short term, as the positive influences are quickly depleted.

Fire Environment/Earth Site

Fire produces Earth, making this a very positive and beneficial situation for those living or working within the Earth site.

Earth Environment/Earth Site

Flat-topped buildings on a flat landscape, or surrounded by similarly shaped buildings, are representative of the double Earth combination. It is considered extremely stable, although unprogressive. The situation is neither beneficial nor harmful. In business terms, success will be sound but undynamic, as there is little to no room for growth or development. In this environment, the function of the site should conform with those surrounding it, that is, either a business in a commercial district or a home in a residential neighborhood.

Metal Environment/Earth Site

A flat-topped building located in the midst of domed structures or surrounded by gently rounded hills is in harmony with its environment. It is not, however, a situation in which a commercial enterprise will thrive. This combination is suitable for a school, hospital, or a family residence where emphasis is placed on community service.

Water Environment/Earth Site

Earth conquers Water, and Earth-type sites are said to feed off their environment. While this combination bodes success, it is at the expense of its surroundings. Here we see advancement in business, career, and social status and the sacrifice of love, respect, and lasting friendship.

——— The Metal Site ———

The architectural attributes of the Metal element—domed roofs and other prominent curved features—are typically found in public institutions such as libraries and museums and in commercial buildings such as banks and other financial houses.

Wood Environment/Metal Site

Metal destroys Wood, and any financial institution housed in a Metal-shaped building will prosper when located in a Wood environment.

Fire Environment/Metal Site

Fire destroys Metal; this combination is not conducive to financial success or security for either business or household.

Earth Environment/Metal Site

Earth and Metal in are the Generative Order, with Earth producing Metal, and this combination guarantees financial success and wealth.

Metal Environment/Metal Site

The Metal element is seen in gently rounded hills and in rounded, domed, and arched buildings. Except in Northern Africa and the Middle East, this kind of building is rarely encountered. Suffice it to say that all same-element combinations should conform in function to the buildings around them.

Water Environment/Metal Site

Metal generates Water. This is a bad combination for a financial institution, as money will continually be lost, flowing away, as it were. It is, however, ideal for a religious center or media organization, since Metal represents wealth and Water the transmission of ideas and information to the world.

—————— The Water Site ——————

The Water-type building has "no shape and every shape" and may appear to have grown over a period of time without any overall plan or design as extensions and modifications were added. Examples of this type of structure are Gaudi's Sagrada Familia Cathedral in Barcelona and the Sydney Opera House. Water-element buildings are distinguished by their asymmetry and irregularity, a fluid shape, and the use of Water-type materials such as glass.

Wood Environment/Water Site

Water feeds Wood, putting these two elements in harmony. Be-

cause the surrounding neighborhood is said to gain from the
Water site, it is recommended that the building be used in a way
that benefits the community.

Fire Environment/Water Site

Here, the Fire element is destroyed by the Water element of the
site. With this combination, the building will function to the
detriment of its surroundings, and its occupants will be resented
by and unwelcome in the community.

Earth Environment/Water Site

As Earth and Water are in the Destructive Order, such a combination is considered harmful. Earth pollutes Water. The meaning here is that those working or living in such a location will
suffer from having their reputations maligned and will experience the ill will of those around them.

Metal Environment/Water Site

This is an extremely fortuitous situation for both commercial enterprises and residential premises. As Metal generates Water, this
means the accumulation of wealth and continued prosperity.

Water Environment/Water Site

Water-type buildings tend to be rare, and a Water environment
usually indicates the actual presence of water. This represents a
both stable and flexible situation, maintaining itself through

constant adaptability. A commercial enterprise will prosper by meeting the changing needs of the consumer, while a home under these auspices will see many generations of the same family raised under its roof.

CHANGING YOUR CIRCUMSTANCES

When a site belongs to an element situated in an environment that is harmful to it, a controlling element can be introduced to alleviate the situation. The controlling element can either destroy the harmful element or generate more of the element that is under attack.

For example, a Wood-type building in a Metal environment (say, a tall wooden structure surrounded by domed or arched buildings or dome-shaped hills) is in the Destructive Order. Wood is under threat from Metal. The situation can be remedied by introducing either a Fire element (an object with the characteristic pointed Fire shape, or even Fire itself, such as a candle or lamp), which destroys Metal; or by introducing Water, such as a pond or fountain, which generates Wood. Another example would be a Fire building (one with a steeply sloped roof) in a Water environment. Water destroys Fire. The Fire building can be protected by introducing a Wood element into the site (such as the planting of trees), which generates Fire, the element under threat, or by introducing an Earth element (such as pottery or a rock garden), which destroys Water.

In the situation where Wood is the threatening element, the Feng Shui master will often introduce a bowl of goldfish. An odd number of fish is usually employed. The color of the fish is bright orange or red, symbolizing Fire. Here two controlling elements are introduced—Fire and Water.

WATER PATTERNS IN THE ENVIRONMENT

An important element of the Form School of Feng Shui is the study of water patterns. Mountain is yin and water is yang. The coupling of yin and yang gives birth to all things. Water that flows toward a mountain feeds the mountain's *chi* and enhances it. Water that flows away from a mountain drains its energy. The mountain helps water to gather *chi*. Thus mountain and water complement each other and give power to a place.

In Feng Shui, water is evaluated by the shape of the particular body of water (river, lake) and by its surface patterns, which are formed by currents, wind, and differences in coloration. Water in which distinct and animated flow patterns can be seen is said to have Water Dragon formations. (Some of the names given to Water Dragon formations are "Coiled Dragon," "Dragon turning back," and "Four Dragons playing with a pearl.") Here, as is so often the case in Feng Shui, one must use a keen sense of observation enhanced by an intuitive and visual imagination in discerning shapes in the natural environment. Like Dragon veins in mountains, Water Dragons are paths of power. Water with no such coherent surface patterns is incapable of collecting and emanating *chi,* and water with no patterns at all is "dead" water, utterly devoid of energy.

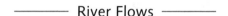

River Flows

Rivers flowing toward a site carry energy to it; those that flow away from the site carry energy away. In rivers with Water Dragons, the tail of the Dragon will face the source (upstream), and the head will face the mouth (downstream).

Coastal Formations

Dragon formations in coastal waters are usually created by the wind. Waters that crash violently onto the shore are destructive; waters that come gently to the land are nourishing. Islands and inlets often contain water energy, but where the coast opens straight onto the sea the energy is dissipated.

Wind and Water

Gentle breezes are benevolent. Gentle winds can create Dragon formations in water, but these same beneficial water patterns can be destroyed by strong winds. Strong winds are harmful carriers of *sha*.

Land that is sheltered from strong winds is protected against such harmful energy. Sheltered waters that are stirred by gentle breezes hold nourishing energy. Land that is subjected to regulated wind flow will be nourished by the wind.

Open land cannot gather wind energy, but land that is totally blocked from the wind is stagnant. Seas and lakes that are constantly whipped by the wind hold no beneficial energy.

——— Fundamental Water Dragon Principles ———

In Chinese thought, as in ancient Druid belief, the Dragon is the symbol of the secret, animated, and creative energy of the universe, and is seen in clouds, earth forms, and in bodies of water. The great philosopher of the Ming Dynasty, Chiang Ping Chieh, classified hundreds of different "dragon patterns" in his book, *The Water Dragon Classic,* which showed the best sites for building near water.

A body of water in the front of a site is considered highly desirable. A small pond specially constructed for this purpose is called the *Ming T'ang;* it serves to ensure that there is a flat, open area in front of the house, one of the basic criteria of the ideal setting.

Water often symbolizes money, and water flowing at an angle toward the site will bring wealth to those who live or work there. Water should not flow in a straight line directly toward a site, as it then becomes a carrier of negative *sha.* If water does flow toward a site, and flows around it, its effects are highly beneficial. The same is true of water that flows directly toward a site but then turns away from it.

Water that flows away from a site should not be visible and ideally should go into the ground or under a bridge.

Water that flows from the Tortoise direction along the Tiger side of the site and then turns and flows along the front (Red Raven) is deemed to bring great good fortune. It only remains for the water flowing away from the site to be invisible for such a combination to constitute an ideal setting.

Water flowing toward a site and then turning to form a deep pool through which the water flows signifies the accumulation of great wealth.

Flowing water carries vigorous *chi,* and where one stream flows into another the *chi* is greatly enhanced. Conversely, where a stream divides, the *chi* is also divided, and the benefits on either side are diminished. But an islet surrounded by water receives the maximum benefit of the *chi* on all sides.

SELECTING A LOCATION

The first priority in selecting a place to live is protection. In Feng Shui, this means safety from harmful elements that affect health, well-being, livelihood, and relationships. A well-protected site has its front, back, and sides guarded by formations that are either natural or artificial and represent the four protectors: Green Dragon, White Tiger, Red Raven, and Black Tortoise. The Green Dragon and the White Tiger, as has already been stipulated, are to the left and right of the site. Land or buildings should be higher than the site and cradle it like arms in an embrace.

Land or buildings to the back (the Black Tortoise) should be higher than the site. If the Black Tortoise is a natural landform, it should be perfectly straight but sloping gently toward the site.

Land to the front (the Red Raven) should be open, but the horizon should not be empty. The site should face a Red Raven formation and be cushioned by layers of hills or buildings. The more layers, the better the protection.

Land should slope away gently from the front of the site, but should not slope away from the back. The back should give a feeling of security and support. However, the back should not be too close to the Black Tortoise formation. If it is, the guardian becomes more intimidator than protector.

A site should never be situated on top of the Green Dragon (the Dragon's Horn) or the White Tiger. These locations are too exposed to the destructive *sha* that the Dragon and the Tiger are meant to shield against.

Never live on a slope without protective vegetation, or atop a crag, ridge, or mountain. These are sites without protection on any side. Similarly, do not live in a house at the edge of or against a cliff, where you appear to be either pushed to the brink or up against a wall.

Certain objects are believed to funnel or focus harmful energy toward a site. Sharp objects such as large tree branches and jagged rocks pointing at a site aim destructive energy at it. Other harmful objects are transformers on power lines, transmitters, construction cranes, and antennas. Sharp objects should never point at the front door or bedroom window of a house. Images of sharp or pointed objects (such as may be seen on advertising billboards) that point directly at the site are harmful.

Large objects that overlook the site and dwarf it compete with the site for energy and, being larger, will absorb all the energy from the area.

Shiny objects collect *sha* and can direct it toward the site. These include sunlight reflected from a glass window, solar panels, reflective light from a nearby body of water, and light reflected off metal objects.

Certain light patterns and shadows can be malevolent. Patterns reflected on a wall that resemble flames, waves, and sharp or pointed objects are harmful.

Any large object located in front of the door prevents *chi* from entering the house and blocks the inhabitants' "way," meaning that obstacles will be met in all undertakings.

Benevolent objects include small bodies of water like ponds

or fountains located in front of a site and round objects such as smooth polished rocks near a site. These provide nourishing energy.

DESTRUCTIVE AND BENEVOLENT STRUCTURES

The sharp corners of buildings and rocky slopes with sharp thin edges oriented toward a site are said to "cut" into the site and are extremely harmful.

A structure with a shiny surface like glass or metal (often found in skyscrapers) is a collector of destructive *sha* that can be directed at the site if the structure is facing it.

Outcrops of rocks, bare escarpments, and cliffs are all harsh-looking structures that contain *sha* and should never face or overlook a site.

Horizontal structures that look like they are cutting into a site are harmful. These can include bridges, power lines, elevated freeways, and mesas, buttes, and flat-topped hills. Triangular-shaped buildings and buildings with protruding sections pointing at the site are also harmful.

Structures that rise vertically in front of or behind a site, seeming to tower threateningly over it, are another source of maleficent energy. A rock formation hanging over a site gives the impression that the site is about to be crushed, and is a source of destructive energy.

Roads and rivers can gather, conduct, and disperse energy according to their pattern. They may be benevolent or malignant depending on their configuration and relationship to a location. In an urban or suburban environment, evaluating road patterns is crucial in choosing a location for a site.

Destructive road patterns carry *sha* to a site and are associated with ill health, family strife, failure, bankruptcy, betrayal, and death. These negative effects are heightened by increased traffic flow and are lessened when traffic is light.

A road that terminates or intrudes into a site is destructive. Therefore sites located at dead ends, T- and Y-junctions, and sharp turns are to be avoided.

Sites located between two parallel roads or those situated between two converging roads or on the corner of an intersection are all equally undesirable.

A road that veers sharply around a site is destructive, as is a road that circles around a house like a noose, strangling it. Sites near bridges, viaducts, and highway interchanges are constantly buffeted by destructive *sha*.

A road running downhill directly toward a site carries harmful energy to it. The energy rushing down toward a house located along a steep road will bring instability to those who reside there, with ill effects on both health and fortune. Mazelike roadways obstruct the flow of *chi* and trap destructive *sha* within the area.

Benevolent road patterns are conveyors of beneficial *chi,* which is associated with harmony, health, well-being, prosperity, and good relations. Dirt and gravel roads carry energy better than paved roads.

A road that cradles a site without winding around it is a conduit of benevolent *chi,* as are roads that resemble river courses with Dragon formations and gentle winding streets.

A site that is situated at the end of a series of loops in a winding road is highly desirable.

BRIDGES

Bridges are generally regarded as potentially dangerous conveyors of *sha.* In China, a common means of averting the threat was to erect a stone slab that faced the bridge. On the stone slab was carved the sentence "The Stone Dares to Resist," along with ornamental tiger heads or the name of the sacred mountain *T'ai Shan.*

TRAFFIC FLOW AND WATER FLOW

Energy that rushes toward, away from, or along the perimeter of a site is destructive energy. This applies equally to traffic and to water flow. Therefore, a site should never be located at the top or bottom of a waterfall, or at the top or bottom of a road that traverses a steep hill. Increased traffic flow along the road increases the negative *sha*.

Similarly, a site should never be located beside a fast-flowing or whitewater stream. Fast-flowing waters are yin in nature and destructive. The same applies to a site along a road with fast-moving traffic, or one located at the end of a busy street.

LAND USE SURROUNDING THE SITE

The use of the land around your building is of particular importance, as land use affects the flow of energy in an area. Land use that is associated with illness, death, violence, and decay brings destructive *sha* to the area, while land that is used for cultivation, healing, learning, spiritual growth, and harmonious interactions has a nourishing effect on the surroundings.

Do not live in a house in the vicinity of a graveyard or mortuary (which create and enhance yin—death—energy). A house next to a hospital or hospice is believed to bring misfortune to its occupants. Electrical generators distort the natural flow of energy in an area and create a vortex of negative energy; a house located near a power station should be avoided.

Do not live in houses near police stations, prisons, or any other facilities dealing with violence or crime, as they are chronic sources of destructive energy.

Do not live near a garbage dump, as waste products harbor death energy that can permeate your house.

Meat-packing plants, slaughterhouses, and tanneries are associated with killing and are sources of violent energy. Any proximity to them is highly undesirable.

The most desirable kind of land is, of course, that which has been left to nature. Forests, woods, and grasslands with abundant wildlife are by far the most ideal environments, where the energy of the place is least likely to have been disturbed. Given that other landform factors are favorable, houses built in these locations will have the best Feng Shui.

Agricultural regions represent the next best type of land use and have extremely beneficial Feng Shui, as the land is used for cultivation and growth.

In an urban or suburban area, a location near a park or gardens, especially when water is present, is highly beneficial, as is being near a playground; the presence of children brings life energy to an area. Being located near a place of healing other than a hospital (for example, an acupuncture clinic or herbalist) or near to a spiritual training center is also beneficial. Places where there is harmonious interaction among people are highly desirable. These include community centers, public squares, churches, schools, and even restaurants and stores where there is joyful and vital interplay between people, which generates nourishing energy.

Generally speaking, what is good Feng Shui for the home also applies to business. There are, however, certain special considerations in choosing a location where a business will be successful.

A good location for a business is, naturally, a shopping plaza (but not at the entrance) or a street with a good flow pattern. Along the rim of a circular traffic way is preferable.

No business should have its door facing a four-way intersection. This is a conduit of negative *sha,* which is further enhanced by the traffic crisscrossing the area.

Fast, heavy traffic is adverse to business. On the other hand, low traffic does not give business enough exposure. As always with the Tao, the middle way is the key to success. Therefore, it's preferable for a business to be located on a street with moderate traffic, but not a street where traffic is dense or fast. This may bring in short-term profit, but it will not last. In this situation, a large parking lot between the store and the busy street can act as a buffer against the negative influences of heavy traffic.

An arcade with a high roof supported by long thin posts is an undesirable location, the belief here being that thinness of support brings thinness of profits.

Anything that breaks up a smooth surface that reflects on the site is beneficial. Terraces, awnings, balconies, and verandahs on the buildings surrounding the site make for a desirable location. It's very good for any office building to have a fountain outside. Awnings are also considered good, especially for retail businesses, as they provide a shield against negative energy, and they collect positive energy.

To have an office in a pyramid-shaped building is considered highly inauspicious. The triangular shape traps malevolent energy and hampers the flow of positive energy, especially in the upper floors. An office should also not be located above a garage, as the negative *sha* generated by the movements of cars is believed to have a very bad effect on business.

Small retail businesses should not have floor-to-ceiling glass windows. When the business is too exposed, profits, like *chi,* leak out. If there are large glass windows, they should be covered by blinds so that exposure is regulated.

Don't have your office in a building with windows that reflect. Wealth and prosperity, it is believed, cannot enter a reflective building.

Don't have your office in a building where the upper levels are larger than the lower. This forebodes the collapse of your business, or an unhappy and destabilizing inequality between the upper executives and middle and lower management and workers.

Don't have an office in a building whose elevators face the front entrance. Negative *sha* enter the elevator and can be carried upward throughout the entire building.

Don't have your business in an office that is located at the end of a hallway.

Don't despair if you have discovered bad Feng Shui in the environment of your home or office. As we saw earlier, the danger can be offset or diminished by introducing a third "controlling" element. This same rule applies when there is a menacing external feature that belongs to a particular element.

When there is only one threatening element, the element that is introduced should be one that destroys the threatening element. Or two elements can be introduced: *one that produces the element under attack* (in the Generative Order) and *one that is threatened by it* (in the Destructive Order).

———— Introducing a Threatening Element ————

Wood

Lamp posts and telegraph poles, and trees outside a front or south-facing window can represent Wood-type threats to a site. Destroying element: Metal.

This is one of the most common types of Feng Shui threats and is traditionally countered by the presence of goldfish in a bowl. Water generates Wood, which would actually seem to increase the threat, but the goldfish represent Fire, which is generated by Wood. Thus the three elements are balanced (known as the "compound-element" remedy). Another more simple remedy would be the strategic placement of a metal object, such as a rounded metal sculpture or a large metal urn.

Fire

The Fire element is seen in pointed roofs and spires. Destroying element: Water.

When Fire threatens a room or site, fountains, water dispensers, or a bowl containing fish other than goldfish can be introduced as countermeasures. The compound elements are Wood (generating Fire) and Earth (generated by Fire), which are readily introduced in the form of a potted plant.

Earth

A flat roof that cuts across the view from a window or other flat horizontal forms produce Earth-type *sha*. Destroying element: Wood. The compound-element remedy is that of Fire and Metal (for example, a candle in a metal holder or a metal lamp).

Metal

Here, the single-element remedy is found in Fire, such as a strategically located fireplace, the always useful red goldfish, or a Fire-shaped object. The compound or two-element remedy combines Earth and Water (for example, a water garden or fountain or pond of stones and water).

Water

Water-type threats can come from electrical installations as well as hostile water patterns. The destroying element remedy is Earth, represented by large stone, clay, or ceramic ornaments and pottery positioned in a way that directly counters the threat. The two-element remedy is found in Metal and Wood, which can be represented by any number of objects made from these two materials.

Introducing a Controlling Element

To correct an imbalance when the element of the surroundings threatens that of the site, one can introduce a controlling element.

Controlling Element: Wood

Wood is represented by tall column-like shapes, plant life, and the color green. Wood is introduced when Fire is under threat from Water (a Fire-type structure in a Water environment) or Water is being threatened by Earth (an irregular, Water-type structure on a flat plane or surrounded by low, flat-topped hills). In these situations, the Feng Shui master may advise placing indoor plants, a wooden statue or screen, or a green decoration in a suitable location. Externally, the planting of tall evergreen trees at the back of the site (never in the front) is a common solution.

Controlling Element: Fire

Fire is represented by sharp angles, the color red, and fire itself. Fire is introduced when Earth is threatened by Wood (a low, flat-roofed Earth-type building surrounded by tall, Wood-type structures) or Wood is threatened by Metal (a Wood-type structure directly threatened by a domed building or low, rounded hills). Fire can be introduced with bright red decorations, such as curtains, floor coverings, or upholstery, or the placement of the core of the heating system or fireplace in a key location.

Controlling Element: Earth

Earth is introduced when Metal is threatened by Fire (a domed structure surrounded by or facing buildings or hills of the Fire shape) or Fire is threatened by Water (a building with steeply sloped roof beside a lake or river). In these instances, the Feng Shui master might suggest an ornamental wall, a sand garden, or the placing of ornamental ceramic ware in a strategic location. Yellow ochre and yellow ochre decorations also represent the Earth element.

Controlling Element: Metal

Metal is introduced when Water is threatened by Earth (a Water-type structure of a flowing or irregular shape, say, with an abundance of glass, facing flat-roofed square buildings of the Earth-shape) or when Earth (a flat-roofed, square building) is threatened by Wood (tall, upright trees, soaring hills, pillars, factory chimneys, or narrow skyscrapers). Metal is represented by the color white, and one of the simplest ways of introducing the Metal element is with a coat of white paint. Wrought iron railings and metal sculptures and ornaments are another means of introducing the Metal element.

Controlling Element: Water

Water is introduced when Wood is under threat from Metal (a tall, narrow structure facing a domed building or surrounded by low, rounded hills), or when Metal (a domed structure) is under threat from Fire (sharp mountain peaks, buildings with pointed roofs, church spires, flame-shaped reflections, or even billboards with images of something burning).

Aquatic plants (a Wood-Water combination), fountains, fish tanks, and even washing facilities are a means of strategically introducing the Water element.

three

CREATING GOOD FENG SHUI
INSIDE YOUR HOME OR OFFICE

The interior of a building, be it commercial or residential, can affect the health and prosperity of its occupants.

In the case of a house, the internal environment includes the shape of the building and its frontage, the floor plan, the interior structures, the front and back yards, the driveway, and the material used for construction. In commercial or apartment buildings, the internal environment consists of the layout of the hallways, the floor plan of the entire building, and the position of the office or unit in relation to the rest of the complex.

Generally, what is good for a house is also good for a business. However, special considerations must be taken into account in the case of business and apartment buildings.

HOUSES

The first and most important consideration in evaluating the interior of a house is its shape. Here three fundamental principles apply: stability, balance, and smoothness.

A stable shape ensures stability of health and livelihood. A building is stable when its upper levels are resting on a solid foundation; it is balanced when none of its levels is disproportionately larger than the rest, and when the levels themselves can be said to "stack" up in a solid way.

Balance means harmony in the household, and a house is balanced if it does not have an irregular shape. Buildings are said to be irregular when they are L- or H-shaped, triangular, or pyramidal; when sections of the house (even though they may be connected by a covered walkway) are cut off or separated from the rest of the house; or when rooms protrude from the main structure.

Smoothness means the absence of harsh surfaces and protruding structures. A house with a uniform surface provides better protection against destructive energy.

Sha is carried in the sharpness of a triangle; a house that has a triangular shape is particularly undesirable. *Sha* collects in the apexes and is unable to escape. The triangular shape also adversely affects the occupants by appearing to press down on them from all sides, creating a feeling of restriction.

Houses that have an irregular shape with sections that jut out—such as buttresses or bedrooms or sunrooms that protrude from the side of the building—are considered unbalanced and harsh, especially when the structures on the upper level are large. Such buildings are also to be avoided.

Round and rectangular-shaped buildings are considered balanced and stable. The round shape smoothes out harsh energy, and rectangular and symmetrical shapes do not allow destructive *sha* to accumulate.

A house with leaning walls creates a very strong visual impression of instability; it looks as though it is about to collapse. Those living in it are in danger of bankruptcy or unemployment.

Long, thin structures extending upward from the building not only make it irregular but are magnets, like lightning rods, for destructive *sha*. This also applies to chimneys that protrude like narrow towers.

You should never live in a house that looks like a military fort or castle. In such a house, you are bound to meet with armed violence, or family members will be injured or even killed in a war.

Don't live in a house that has structures resembling equipment or machinery associated with death, such as a house that has a framelike structure in the front that resembles a gallows.

Don't live in a house that looks like a crag, as craggy landforms are yin and carry *sha*.

Don't live in a house that resembles cards stacked on their edges. This is an extremely unstable structure (in Feng Shui terms) and forebodes the collapse of the occupants' fortunes.

If you live in a house that looks like it is being crushed by a large object, you will be dominated by others and your business ventures will fail.

Don't live in a house surrounded by pillars. Pillars give the impression that the structure is confined, or "jailed," and its occupants will be either physically, mentally, or financially constricted.

Roofs

A dome-shaped roof or skylight is highly desirable. Roundness collects *chi* and is the best protector against destructive *sha*.

Small areas such as dormer windows protruding from the roof of a house make for an irregular design, which is most undesirable.

In an A-frame house, the roof should not be too steep, as this creates a harsh triangular structure.

A roof that slopes all the way to the ground forms a heavy lid that prevents nourishing *chi* from entering the building.

A "cascading" roof on a house, that is, a roof that descends like steps in a series of different horizontal levels, gives the impression that the stucture is falling or sliding away, and those who dwell beneath it are bound to lose money in their investments and business transactions.

Foundations

Although it may be stable from an engineering point of view, a house in which the upper levels are larger than the lower is, in Feng Shui terms, top heavy and therefore unstable (note the use of "visual" criteria as opposed to "scientific," as is so often the case in Feng Shui).

If a house or apartment is composed of several levels, they should all be roughly the same size. This makes the house balanced. If there is a discrepancy in size, the upper levels should be smaller, although not too much so. If the upper levels are proportionately too small, then the structure is considered unbalanced.

Houses supported by posts or pillars are unstable.

A house built on a slope with, say, its front supported by posts, is also considered unstable.

─────── Floor Plan ───────

A house that has a balanced and stable shape may still have a floor plan that is not conducive to harmonious and healthy living, because various interior elements also affect energy flow.

The Entrance

The entrance is an important determinant of the Feng Shui of a house. It is the portal through which positive *chi* or negative *sha* enters and affects the general welfare of the occupants.

The front door should always open inward and should not open onto a narrow corridor or passageway; otherwise the flow of *chi* to the rest of the house is restricted, and negative *sha* gets trapped in the entranceway. Nor should the entrance be funneled from outside of the door (that is, flanked by the walls of structures protruding from the house). This type of entrance gathers negative energy and focuses it on the house.

The entrance should open into a foyer that buffers the rest of the house from the outside. This allows nourishing *chi* to collect and be distributed throughout the rest of the building. Also, if malevolent *sha* does enter, the foyer is there to absorb or dilute the negative energy, lessening its effect on the rest of the house.

The foyer should not be walled on all sides with only one doorway into the rest of the house. Positive energy will be constricted and negative energy trapped.

Corridors

A house should not have too many corridors. The arrangement of the corridors determines whether a house has good circulation that allows *chi* to pass through or traps negative *sha*.

Long winding corridors are undesirable, as they can transform positive *chi* into a twisting and unmanageable form of *sha*.

The door of a room should not open onto a long corridor. Long corridors compress energy, once again turning *chi* into *sha,* and such doors enable *sha* to enter the rooms.

Corridors should be well lit, as dark, gloomy areas collect yin, or death, energy. Doors opening onto corridors should reveal windows to the outside that allow yang energy from the sun to enter.

Stairways

Spiral staircases enhance malevolent energy, because energy that is forced to twist as it rises becomes destructive.

Narrow stairways leading straight up with only a narrow landing at each floor are also undesirable, as the gradient of the ascending and descending energy is too steep. Energy rushing through a long narrow stairway is wild and unpredictable, like wind in a wind tunnel, and is too often destructive.

Wide and shallow stairs facilitate the gentle flow of *chi*. Steep steps in a staircase are highly undesirable.

Generally, stairs should not directly face the front door.

Bedrooms

The bedroom should be regular and symmetrical and therefore conducive to the flow of gentle and beneficial *chi*. It should have only one door. Sleeping is a means of replenishing energy, and if there is more than one entrance then nourishing *chi* that might otherwise be absorbed can flow out of the room.

The ceiling should not be triangular in shape, which traps negative energy, the danger of which is enhanced while one is sleeping.

The bedroom door should not face a stairway. Destructive *sha* rushing up the stairs will directly enter the room.

It is inauspicious to have beams over the head of the sleeper. If the room is small and an overhead beam is unavoidable, the bed should be positioned so that the beam runs the length of the bed rather than across it.

The Kitchen

The kitchen should be shielded from the front entrance, and thus guarded from any malevolent energy that enters through the front door. Ideally, it should be centrally located and sheltered by the rest of the house, and have more than one doorway to ensure good circulation. Its shape should be regular and symmetrical so that no pockets of negative energy can accumulate. It should also be aligned on a central axis with the house and not diagonal to it, so that *chi* is able to flow easily to it. Also, you should ensure that the stove (representing the Wood element) does not adjoin either a Water or Wood element. Being next to Wood enhances the danger of Fire, while being next to Water produces a combination that in Chinese characters spells "disaster."

The Garage

Ideally, the garage should be separate from the house because the movement of cars disrupts the flow of energy in the house. Vehicular movement also carries destructive *sha*. Having the garage separated from the house prevents the negative energy spreading into the rest of the home. For the same reasons, the residential part of the house should not be situated above a garage. A room that is frequently used, such as a bedroom, living room, or kitchen, should never be located at the back of the garage. It is as though the car is about to run down the occupants of the house, and it is believed those living in such an arrangement will often be ill or even involved in road accidents.

 General Floor Plan

The front and back doors should not be lined up or in view of each other. Otherwise, *chi* entering through the front will flow straight out through the back.

Corridors should not feel cramped or constricted, as this inhibits the flow of *chi*.

Split-level houses are considered highly undesirable. Feng Shui masters hold that if the front half of the house is higher than the back, children will have difficulty in achieving independence. If the back is higher than the front, the family wealth will be dissipated.

The arrangement of levels and rooms should be as regular as possible. Irregularity confuses the flow of energy, and transforms beneficial *chi* into harmful *sha*.

All rooms should receive adequate natural light (yang or life energy). A dark house traps yin or death energy. No part of the house should require artificial light when the sun is shining. However, windows should not be huge. A house with large windows or glass walls has very poor protection against destructive *sha* and can leak nourishing *chi*.

Flat, arched, vaulted, and dome-shaped ceilings are the most desirable. Energy circulation will be even if the ceiling is flat and enhanced if the ceiling is vaulted.

Triangular or sloping ceilings constrict the flow of nourishing energy and gather destructive *sha*. Nor should ceilings be too high; *chi* rises and will be trapped at the top. Ceilings that are uneven in height disrupt the circulation of energy and are also undesirable.

A study or office should not have a door in direct line with an exit from the house. As they are places of work, success and prosperity will flow away. Rooms frequently used by all the members of the household should not have doors aligned with any door leading outside. Bedrooms, also, should not have doors opening directly to the outside.

———— Frontage and Driveway ————

The frontage and driveway act as buffers between the house and the external environment. Depending on their arrangement, they can improve or damage the Feng Shui of a house.

The backyard should always be larger than the front.

Round structures like fountains, ponds, and gazebos are highly desirable in both front and back yards.

The driveway should never run directly toward the house. Circular driveways are the most desirable. The driveway of the house across the street should not point directly at the front door, nor should there be a long narrow path leading straight to it. Trees should never block the front door. Paths and driveways should preferably be of dirt or gravel. An unpaved driveway enhances nourishing Earth energy and effectively cushions any negative *sha*.

Fences with sharp points are highly undesirable.

Buffers between the house and the street are always desirable. Front porches, gardens, terraces, and trellises all protect the residence from destructive energy and promote the presence of nourishing *chi*.

────── Decks, Landings, Verandahs, and Bridges ──────

Circular-shaped decks are considered best, and should be supported by strong posts. Structures on decks, such as hot tubs, are also best when round.

Verandahs on upper levels, also, should be supported by strong, thick pillars.

In Chinese tradition, bridges and pathways are associated with departure. Therefore, it is unwise to have a bridge or covered walkway connecting two houses or sections of a house. This will cause separation within the household. Married couples will divorce, family relationships will be strained or fractured, and children will leave home early.

Exposed beams inside a house create negative *sha,* as they can appear to be threatening to crush the inhabitants. If there are overhead beams, say, in the living or dining rooms, seating should be arranged so that there are no beams directly over any of the chairs.

Fireplaces and woodstoves should not dominate a room, because they enhance the presence of the Fire element in the house.

Vertical blinds are undesirable. When opened, they resemble blades cutting into the room.

Lights that cast spotted and broken shadows are also harmful, giving the impression that yin (darkness, decay, and death) is in conflict with or even dominating yang (light and life).

Wooden doors and paneling should not have knotty or gnarly patterns that are excessive or harsh-looking. Such patterns disturb the flow of energy.

APARTMENTS

Most of the Feng Shui principles relating to houses carry over to apartments. Here are a few particulars:

Do not live in an apartment building with long hallways, where the stairs are not buffered by a landing or where the landings on each floor are narrow.

Do not live in a unit that is next to or has a door facing the elevator or stairs, nor in a unit that is at the end of a hallway with a corridor running into it.

DEFLECTING *SHA* AND ENHANCING *CHI*

Mirrors are the most common interior means by which *chi* is enhanced and adverse *sha* deflected. Mirrors should be positioned in areas where the flow of *chi* comes to a dead end. Mirrors can also be strategically placed so as to deflect the onslaught of "secret arrows" directed at the room or site. "Secret arrows," you will recall, are a special kind of *sha* that is "shot" from the hard corners of a building or a sharp bend in a road pointing at an angle at the site. A *sha*-deflecting mirror will reflect the baleful image back at itself while at the same time revealing some other more benign scene, perhaps water or some feature of a garden.

Mirrors intended to enhance the flow of *chi* should be placed at an angle, so that the path of the *chi* is directed further along its way. Mirrors meant to counter *sha* should reflect it straight back out of the house.

Sound is also another means of deflecting *sha*. Wind chimes, the soothing sound of running water, or any melodic, pleasing sound, like Chinese songbirds, are all effective protectors.

Harmonious and gentle colors also soothe or diminish disruptive *sha,* as does adequate lighting. The presence of anything living—fish (always have an odd number), plants, a bird, even a dog or a cat—helps in warding off the effects of *sha*. However, avoid plants with sharp spiky leaves.

Banners, flags, wind chimes, mobiles—anything that moves in a breeze—activate and disperse lingering *sha,* as does gently flowing water and smoke from burning incense.

Objects that are beautiful and enhance a sense of stillness and serenity, such as a statue of Buddha, Kwan Yin (the Chinese goddess of compassion and mercy), or the Madonna, or even a piece of driftwood or a particular stone, can exercise a powerful countereffect on intrusive *sha*.

Interestingly enough, according to some modern-thinking Feng Shui practitioners, anything deemed to be a device—such as a television, radio, refrigerator, electrical apparatus, anything used as a tool, including computers and handsaws, and even something as simple as a calendar—can also be used to offset *sha*.

Sha travels in straight lines, and straight objects such as fishing rods, the armrests of chairs, a boat oar, or a bamboo pole can be positioned in such a way as to funnel *sha* away.

four

DETERMINING THE
BEST USE OF EACH ROOM

Feng Shui has a lot to say about the effects the eight compass directions (north, northeast, east, southeast, south, southwest, west, and northwest) have on the interior functioning of a building, and about the effect of the orientation (the direction faced by the front door) of a building. Certain activities are best done in specific locations, depending on the direction and the orientation of the house, apartment, or office. Feng Shui has something to say, for example, about where the kitchen should be in a home or where the business manager's office should be located within a commercial enterprise.

In Feng Shui, each compass point is represented by a trigram. To determine the meaning of the orientation of your home or office, we need first to understand what a trigram is. In Taoist philosophy, all things can be reduced to yin and yang. The trigrams, you may remember, are symbols made up of three horizontal lines that may be broken (yin, with feminine attributes) or unbroken (yang, with masculine attributes), and represent a binary system of mathematics. There are eight possible combinations of yin and yang lines, each with its own name, symbolism, meaning, and effect. They are considered to represent the primary building blocks of the universe.

THE DIRECTIONS OF THE TRIGRAMS

There are two arrangements of the trigrams, the Later Heaven Sequence and the Earlier Heaven Sequence. The Earlier Heaven

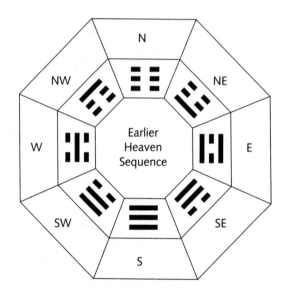

The Eight Trigrams and their directions
in the Earlier and Later Heaven Sequences

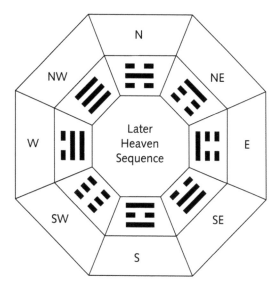

Sequence is usually found on mirrors and talismans to ward off evil *sha,* while the Later Heaven Sequence is the one found on the dials of Chinese mariners' compasses.

You can select the appropriate areas for different activities within the site according to the location and symbolism of each trigram. Besides ruling spheres of activity, the trigrams also represent family relationships and elements. Following is a table of the trigrams, their symbolism, family relationship, quality, directions, and element.

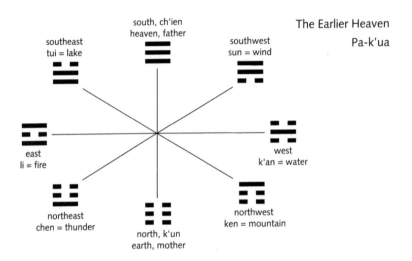

south, ch'ien
heaven, father

southeast
tui = lake

The Earlier Heaven

Pa-k'ua

southwest
sun = wind

east
li = fire

west
k'an = water

northeast
chen = thunder

north, k'un
earth, mother

northwest
ken = mountain

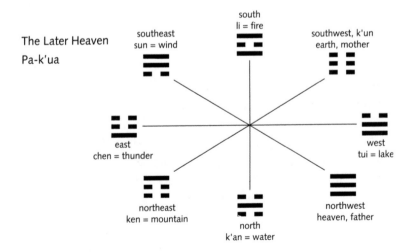

south
li = fire

The Later Heaven

Pa-k'ua

southeast
sun = wind

southwest, k'un
earth, mother

east
chen = thunder

west
tui = lake

northeast
ken = mountain

north
k'an = water

northwest
heaven, father

	Name	Symbol	Family Relationship	Quality	Directions	Element
☰	Ch'ien	Heaven (yang)	Father	Authority	South (Earlier Heaven) / Northwest (Later Heaven)	Metal
☴	Sun	Wind	Eldest Daughter	Growth and Trade	Southwest (Earlier Heaven) / Southeast (Later Heaven)	Wood
☲	Li	Fire	Middle Daughter	Fire	East (Earlier Heaven) / South (Later Heaven)	Fire
☶	Ken	Mountain	Youngest Son	Obstacles	Northwest (Earlier Heaven) / Northeast (Later Heaven)	Earth
☱	Tui	Lake	Youngest Daughter	Joy	Southeast (Earlier Heaven) / West (Later Heaven)	Metal
☵	K'an	Water	Middle Son	Wheels, Danger	West (Earlier Heaven) / North (Later Heaven)	Water
☳	Chen	Thunder	Eldest Son	Speed, Roads	Northeast (Earlier Heaven) / East (Later Heaven)	Wood
☷	K'un	Earth (yin)	Mother	Nourishment	North (Earlier Heaven) / Southwest (Later Heaven)	Earth

The Compass School of Feng Shui classifies buildings into eight principal types according to the direction faced by the front door, and are named according to the trigram of their orientation in the Later Heaven Sequence. Buildings that are not directly aligned are classified according to the nearest direction. Feng Shui also holds that the interior of any building has places that are intrinsically more favorable than others, as well as places that are detrimental to the well-being of anyone living or working in them for prolonged periods.

Favorable and unfavorable areas of a building's interior are determined by the conjunction of trigrams obtained when the Earlier Heaven Sequence is imposed upon the Later Heaven Sequence. The conjunctions, or interaction, of the trigrams for each direction of the environment with those of the site itself result in the Seven Portents (Eight if the entrance is included).

The names of the favorable areas of a house are *Nien Yen,* or Lengthened Years; *Sheng Ch'i,* or Generating Breath; and *T'ien I,* or Celestial Monad. The unfavorable areas are known as *Hai Huo,* Accident and Mishap; *Chüeh Ming,* Severed Fate; *Wu Kuei,* Five Ghosts; and *Liu Sha,* Six Curses.

The following illustrated key to the location of the Seven Portents is taken from their order in the fundamental south-facing or *Li*-type house.

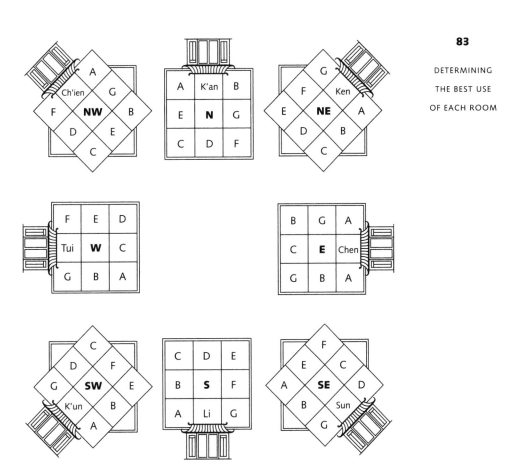

Portents of the Eight Orientations

The basic floor plan

A = Six Curses, B = Five Ghosts, C = Severed Fate, D = Lengthened Years,
E = Accident and Mishap, F = Generating Breath, G = Celestial Monad

The positions of the portents change according to the orientation of the building. When planning which areas of the house to use for work, rest, or leisure, you should consider which direction or location is the most appropriate for the particular kind of activity. There is a slight variation in the way the portents are considered between that of a home and business. For instance, while the Five Ghosts may not be welcome in the bedroom, it may not matter (depending on your point of view) that a work area is haunted (unless you find the presence of ghosts distracting). And while in the house you would like Lengthened Years in the living room or bedroom, in a business this area might be more suitable for ensuring the protection of any valuable or perishable goods, or as the business management or accounting areas.

The following tables show the auguries and the locations of the Seven Portents for each of the different possible orientations of a site. (The orientation of a site is the direction faced by the front door.)

——— Six Curses ———

This area portents an event or minor setback that one has cause to regret seven times. It should be used as a neutral area—storage or a bathroom—as long as precautions are taken, and not, say, as an area where business or family decisions are made or important work carried out.

POSITION OF THE SIX CURSES IN EACH ORIENTATION

Orientation	Six Curses
North	Northwest
Northeast	East
East	Northeast
Southeast	West
South	Southwest
Southwest	South
West	Southeast
Northwest	North

——— Five Ghosts ———

The Five Ghosts are the spirits of people who have died, as distinct from nonhuman supernatural beings. This area will have a haunted quality, and in a Chinese household would be reserved for a memorial to the family's ancestors or a shrine to protect the premises.

Orientation	Five Ghosts
North	Northeast
Northeast	Southeast
East	Northwest
Southeast	Southwest
South	West
Southwest	Southeast
West	South
Northwest	East

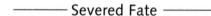

Severed Fate

This is a most inauspicious location, as it refers to the ending of life, and is best used for storage.

POSITION OF SEVERED FATE IN EACH ORIENTATION

Orientation	Severed Fate
North	Southwest
Northeast	South
East	West
Southeast	Northeast
South	Northwest
Southwest	North
West	East
Northwest	South

As its name suggests, this is a most auspicious area, ideal for living, working, sleeping, or recovering from illness.

POSITION OF LENGTHENED YEARS IN EACH ORIENTATION

Orientation	Lengthened Years
North	South
Northeast	Southwest
East	Southeast
Southeast	East
South	North
Southwest	Northwest
West	Northeast
Northwest	Southwest

Accident and Mishap

This area is vulnerable to accidents resulting in physical injury. It is of particular importance that the kitchen never be located in this area (or in Severed Fate). The danger from the Fire element is apparent, while the Metal element threatens mishap from the use of knives and other kitchen utensils.

POSITION OF ACCIDENT AND MISHAP IN EACH ORIENTATION

Orientation	Accident and Mishap
North	West
Northeast	West

Orientation	Accident and Mishap
East	Southwest
Southeast	Northwest
South	Northeast
Southwest	East
West	North
Northwest	Southeast

——— Generating Breath ———

This area is filled with vitalizing *chi*, and is ideally suited for any room in which long periods of time are spent, such as a study, office, or creative studio. Like Lengthened Years, it is also a good place to recover from illness or to rejuvenate.

POSITION OF GENERATING BREATH IN EACH ORIENTATION

Orientation	Generating Breath
North	Southeast
Northeast	Northwest
East	South
Southeast	North
South	West
Southwest	Northeast
West	Northwest
Northwest	West

This is a favorable location in which malign *sha* is neutralized and beneficial *chi* is regenerated, having a rejuvenating and cleansing effect on those who occupy the space. This is the ideal spot for the physical, mental, spiritual, and even financial rejuvenation of those who have experienced misfortune or illness.

POSITION OF CELESTIAL MONAD IN EACH ORIENTATION

Orientation	Celestial Monad
North	West
Northeast	North
East	North
Southeast	South
South	Southeast
Southwest	West
West	Southwest
Northwest	Northeast

THE DIRECTION FACED BY THE SITE

The auspices for this location are favorable. Such a location might be a room above the entrance. You can determine who might best use this room by consulting the table of the Eight Trigrams and their family relationships.

The Eight Trigrams or Directions, along with the Seven Portents, can be used in commercial sites to determine which type of activity is best suited to each location within the building. All work means change, and each of the Eight Trigrams represents change in its various stages and forms. First, we will look at the Eight Trigrams or directions.

K'an—North

K'an means circular motion and is the symbol of danger and dangerous activity, and in a business is associated with machinery, drills, circular saws, and the like.

Ken—Northeast

Ken means barriers and immutability, and this area is ideally suited as a security zone or for the storage of valuable items.

Chen—East

Chen also means change of place, and is therefore associated with transport and distribution, making it suitable for dispatch (a mail room) or for production line processes.

Sun—Southeast

Sun means both change of form and continuity, and is suitable for slow, painstaking tasks as well as routine work.

Li—South

Li means fire and change of substance, and is ideal for industrial processes using heat, such as furnaces, kilns, and electrical discharges.

K'un—Southwest

K'un means nourishment and biological change, and is well suited for seed germination and all other biological processes, for instance, the growth of cultures in a laboratory.

Tui—West

Tui indicates psychological or mental change and is best suited to matters concerning entertainment and recreation as well as to scientific instrument calibration and delicate measurement.

Ch'ien—Northwest

Ch'ien is creative change, strength, and expansion, and is ideal for all matters pertaining to creative processes, leadership, and management.

The following sections focus on the Seven Portents and the areas of business activity best suited to each of them. You should consult the tables of the positions occupied by the different portents for each of the eight orientations.

Six Curses

As we have already seen, Six Curses portend repeated setbacks and irritation. In this instance, you should decide which aspect of your business would be least likely to be affected from the influences of the Six Curses (perhaps the restroom, but it is hard to predict *what* the result might be).

Five Ghosts

The Five Ghosts are not likely to be a problem in a business that closes down at night. In China, it was common for a shrine to be placed in this area, not only to appease the spirits but to solicit their cooperation. If numerous inexplicable accidents and incidents keep occurring in this area, the usual course of action would be some form of exorcism, or perhaps an offering to quiet the spirits down, or simply using the area as a storage area or restroom, if having a haunted toilet is something you can live with.

──── Severed Fate ────

This area signifies grave physical danger. It should never be used for any potentially dangerous work or for the use of heavy machinery. Even storage in this area is risky, and if it is so used, items should be stored with the utmost care to avoid injury.

──── Accident and Mishap ────

Another area prone to accident, although not as bad as Severed Fate. Cutting, or any kind of use of sharp implements or other potentially hazardous tasks, should be strictly avoided here.

──── Lengthened Years ────

This area is best used as the director's or manager's office, or for accounting, to ensure the continuing prosperity of your business.

──── Generating Breath ────

If the business is based on simple work to order, then this area should be used for management and accounting. If, on the other hand, the business is based on the generation of new ideas and being up-to-date with the latest advances in its field, then this area should be the heart of the workplace, as, for example, a design studio.

As in a house, this is a generally favorable area. It should be assigned to what you regard as second or third in importance in terms of your business operations, such as routine work, administration, or dispatch.

THE EIGHT ENRICHMENTS

Your home, office, or garden can also be divided into eight areas, known as enrichments, that represent different aspects of your life, with each area generating a different type of *chi*. These eight forms of *chi* correspond with the eight compass directions, and all have their own particular beneficial qualities.

Direction	Enrichment
North	Nurturing *chi*
Northeast	Flourishing *chi*
East	Stimulating *chi*
Southeast	Creative *chi*
South	Vigorous *chi*
Southwest	Soothing *chi*
West	Calming *chi*
Northwest	Expansive *chi*

The area faced by your front door or garden gate is called 1 *Wang T'sai*, Prosperity and Fame. Behind you is 5 *Chin Yin*,

Relationships. To your left is 7 *Fa Chan,* Wisdom and Experience. To your right is 3 *Chan Yin,* Pleasure and Indulgence. To the left of this area is 2 *Pan Lu,* Peace and Happiness. Between 3 and 5 is 4 *Chin T'sai,* New Beginnings. Between 5 and 7 is 6 *T'ien Ch'ai,* Children and Family. Between 7 and 1 is 8 *Huan Lo,* Wealth and Money.

These enrichments can work for your entire house, a single room, office, or even a small work area. Like the Red Raven

The eight enrichments of a house, office, or garden

and Black Tortoise, *Wang T'sai* always corresponds to the direction you face, while *Chin Yin* is always at the back. Ideally, as we have already seen, you are facing south. But if, for instance, you are facing southeast, then you are merely benefiting from a different form of *chi* flowing toward you, in this case *chi* that is creative. It is a good idea to draw up a plan of your room or house and note the locations of the eight enrichments in relation to the *chi* of the eight directions, to see which kinds of activities will benefit the most from each of the areas. Whatever the orientation of the room or house, the area of *Wang T'sai*, Prosperity and Fame, always corresponds to the main entrance. *Wang T'sai,* though, works best if the main entrance is in the south, where the *chi* is vigorous and lively. If the main entrance faces some other direction, then, as we have already stated, the *chi* affecting your area of Prosperity and Fame will be different. If, for instance, *Wang T'sai* is in the west—where the *chi* is calming—prosperity and fame will come to you quietly. Also, with *Wang T'sai* in the west, your *Fa Chan*—Wisdom and Experience—is in the south, where the *chi* is vigorous, perhaps indicating that you will be well traveled, have many adventures, and that knowledge will come to you more from the "school of life" than from the sedentary reading of books.

In business, your *Chin T'sai*—New Beginnings area—would be well used for negotiating new contracts, while *Huan Lo*—Wealth and Money—should naturally be the area where accounting and transactions are handled.

TO LEARN MORE

This book has offered a very basic layperson's introduction to Feng Shui. In the name of simplicity, we have not gone into the more complex aspects of this ancient art and science, such as using the Taoist compass to determine the suitability of a location and design of your home or office building, compiling your Feng Shui horoscope and matching it to your home, or using the Chinese calendar. We hope that this book has stimulated you to want to learn more, and we have compiled a list of suggested reading to aid you in this endeavor.

Govert, Johndennis. *Feng Shui: Art and Harmony of Place.* Phoenix, AZ: Daikakuji Publications, 1993.

Lagatree, Kirsten. *Feng Shui at Work: Arranging Your Work Space to Achieve Peak Performance and Maximum Profit.* New York: Villard Books, 1998.

Lam, Kam Chuen. *Feng Shui Handbook: How to Create a Healthier Living and Working Environment.* New York: Henry Holt, 1996.

Lin, Jami. *The Essence of Feng Shui: Balancing Your Body, Home, and Life with Fragrance.* Carlsbad, CA: Hay House, 1998.

Lin, Jami, and Layna Fischer. *Feng Shui Today: Earth Design, the Added Dimension.* Miami Shores, FL: Earth Design, 1995.

Lip, Evelyn. *Layman's Guide to Chinese Geomancy.* Union City, CA: Heian International, 1987.

____. *Feng Shui for Business.* Union City, CA: Heian International, 1990.

Rossbach, Sarah. *Feng Shui: The Chinese Art of Placement.* New York: Dutton, 1995.

Rossbach, Sarah, and Yun Lin. *Feng Shui Design: From History and Landscape to Modern Gardens and Interiors.* New York: Viking, 1998.

Simons, T. Raphael. *Feng Shui Strategies for Business Success: Arranging Your Office for Success and Prosperity with Personalized Astrological Charts.* New York: Three Rivers Press, 1998.

Too, Lillian. *The Complete Illustrated Guide to Feng Shui: How to Apply the Secrets of Chinese Wisdom for Health, Wealth and Happiness.* Boston: Element, 1996.

____. *Applied Pakua and Loshu Feng Shui.* New York: Weatherhill, 1998.

Walters, Derek. *The Feng Shui Handbook: A Practical Guide to Chinese Geomancy.* London: Thorsons, 1991.

Webster, Richard. *Feng Shui Tips for the Home.* St. Paul, MN: Llewellyn Publications, 1998.

Wu, Ying, Yin Wu, and Paul Davies. *Do-It-Yourself Feng Shui: Take Charge of Your Destiny.* Boston: Element, 1998.

ABOUT THE AUTHOR

Damian Sharp, an Asian studies scholar, was born in Australia and currently resides in San Francisco, California. He is the recipient of two Literary Fellowship Awards from the Australian Council for the Arts. His collection of short stories, *When A Monkey Speaks,* was published in 1994. Mr. Sharp adapted the title story of the collection for a screenplay which is in development for a motion picture. His short stories have appeared in the *Chicago Review* and the *Denver Quarterly,* and he has written for *The Soho Weekly News, Rice Magazine,* and *California Magazine.*

INDEX

Accidents, 71, 82, 84, 87–88, 92–93
accounting, *see* business function
administration, *see* business function
angles, *see* shapes
animals, 7, 19, 21–23, 38, 76
apartments, 35, 63, 67, 74, 77
autumn, *see* seasons

Backyard, 72
balance, 4, 16, 63–64
balcony, *see* structures
bankruptcy, 52, 65
basement, *see* rooms
bedroom, *see* rooms
black, *see* colors
blinds, *see* curtains
Book of Changes, The, see I Ching

Book of Rites, The, see *Li Shu*
Book of t he River Lo, The, see *Lo Shu*
bridge, *see* structures
Buddhism, 3, 76
buildings (*see also* public buildings)
  business, *see* work place
  financial, 34, 41–42
  four sides of, 19
  location of (*see also* site), 22–23
  orientation of, 2, 82–89
  religious, 32, 36, 42, 62
  shape of, 2, 42, 63–64
  warehouse, 34
business function (*see also* work place)
  accounting, 84, 93, 96
  administration, 94
  mailroom, 90, 94

management, 57, 84, 91, 93

Candles, 44, 59
care, *see* nourishment
ceiling, 69, 72
center, *see* directions
chairs, 74, 76
chi, 4, 16, 21, 28–30, 45–46, 48, 50, 53, 57, 66–73, 75, 88–89, 94, 96
  definition of, 28
  enhancing, 75
Chiang Ping Chieh *(see also Water Dragon Classic, The),* 47
Chi Gong, 28
children *(see also* family), 38, 55, 71, 73
chimney, *see* structures
China, 1–3, 5–7, 10, 12, 28–29, 53, 70, 73, 92
Chou Dynasty, 12
Chou-i, 12
colors, 10, 17, 21, 31, 34, 45, 60–62, 75

black, 4, 21, 23, 27, 31, 49, 96
blue, 27
green, 21, 23–24, 27, 31, 49, 60
orange, 45
red, 21, 23, 27, 30–31, 34, 45, 48–49, 59, 61, 95
white, 4, 21, 23–25, 27, 31, 49, 62
yellow, 9–10, 31, 61
column, *see* structures
commerce, *see* professions, commerce; success, commercial
community, 36, 40, 43, 55
Confucianism, 3, 12
creative energy, *see chi;* professions, creative
creativity, 33–34, 36
curtains, 57, 61, 74
cycle of change, 4

Danger, physical, 93
dangerous activities, 90

death, 2, 4, 25, 46, 52, 54–55, 65, 68, 71, 74–75
Destructive Order, 32, 43–44, 58
directions
    center, 31
    east, 19, 21, 25, 31, 77, 81, 85–90, 94
    five, 31
    north, 18–21, 25, 27, 31, 77, 81, 85–90, 94
    northeast, 77, 81, 85–90, 94
    northwest, 77, 81, 85–89, 91, 94
    south, 18–21, 25, 27, 31, 58, 77, 81–82, 85–89, 91, 94, 96
    southeast, 77, 81, 85–89, 91, 94, 96
    southwest, 77, 81, 85–89, 91, 94
    west, 19–21, 25, 31, 77, 81, 85–89, 91, 94, 96
disaster, 19, 70
divorce (*see also* family), 73

doors (*see also* entrance), 28–30, 50, 56, 67–75, 77, 82, 84, 94
Dragon, 17–19, 21, 23–28, 45–47, 49, 53
    and Tiger, 24–27
    breath of the, 23
    chasing the, 23
    formations, 17, 45–47, 53
    salivating pearls, 19
    veins, 23–24, 45
driveway, *see* structures
Duke of Chou (King Wen), 12

Earlier Heaven formations, 17
Earlier Heaven Sequence, 78, 82
Earth, 3, 10–11, 16, 23, 29, 31–35, 39–41, 59–61, 73, 81
    and Fire, 31, 34, 39
    and Metal, 35, 41
    and Water, 41, 43, 59
    and Wood, 37, 39
east, *see* directions
Eight Enrichments, 94–96
    Children and Family, 95

Eight Enrichments *continued*
New Beginnings, 95, 96
Peace and Happiness, 95
Pleasure and Indulgence, 95
Prosperity and Fame, 94, 96
Relationships, 95
Wealth and Money, 95, 96
Wisdom and Experience,
95, 96
Eight Orientations (*see also*
Seven Portents), 82–84
Eight Trigrams (*see also*
pa-k'ua), directions of, 7,
78–80, 90–92
electric devices, 76
elements (*see also* Earth; Fire;
Metal; Water; Wind), 7, 15,
31–45, 58–62, 70, 74, 79,
81, 87
controlling, 44, 60–62
Destructive Order of, 32, 35
five, 31, 33, 35
Generative Order of, 31,
34–35, 41, 58
harmful, 29–30, 43–44,
46–55, 57–58

helping each other, 31
symbolic meaning of, 33
energy, 1–2, 4, 15–18, 21, 23,
25, 28–30, 45–47, 50–55,
57, 64–65, 67–74
benevolent, 18, 51, 55, 57,
68
flow and directions of, 2,
15, 17, 67, 70–71, 74
negative, *see sha*
protective, 23
entrance (*see also* doors), 19,
21, 57, 67–70, 89
environment
Earth, 37, 39–41, 43
Fire, 36, 38–41, 43
harmful, changing of, 44
healthy, 28
Metal, 37, 39–44
Water, 37, 39, 41–44
Wood, 36–39, 41–42

Family, 44, 52, 65, 71, 73,
79, 81, 85, 89, 95
fang-shih (*see also* Feng Shui,
masters; Taoism), 6

fence, *see* structures
Feng Shui
   burial sites and, 2
   Compass School of, 12, 82
   first books on, 12
   Form School of, 12, 45
   literal translation of, 6
   masters (*see also fang-shih*),
     6, 29, 45, 60, 61, 71
Fire, 31–34, 36, 38–41,
   43–45, 58–62, 70, 74, 81,
   87, 91
   and Earth, 34, 59
   and Metal, 39, 41, 59
   and Water, 39, 43, 45
   and Wood, 38
fireplace, 38, 59, 61, 74
fish (*see also* goldfish), 45, 62
floor plans, 67–74, 84
formations (*see also* Earlier
   Heaven formations; Later
   Heaven formations; shapes),
   12, 17, 23, 25, 27, 32,
   45–46, 48–49, 51, 53
   age of, 17
   cliffs, 16, 25, 49, 51
   coastal, 16–17, 46
   forests, 36–37, 55
   fountains, 17, 44, 56, 59,
     62, 72
   gullies, 25, 29
   hills, 12, 18, 25, 27–28,
     32–33, 37, 40, 42, 49,
     51, 54, 60–62
   lakes, 37, 44–45, 47, 59,
     61, 81
   mountains, 12–13, 15–18,
     23–25, 32–33, 36–37,
     45, 49, 62, 81
   rivers, 13, 37, 45–46, 48,
     52–54, 61
   Water Dragon, 45–47
   waterfalls, 54
foundations, 66–67
friendship, 41
Fu Hsi (*see also* shaman-
   kings), 7, 11

Garage, *see* rooms
garden, *see* structures
Generative Order, 31, 34–35,
   41, 58

goldfish, 45, 58–59
Great Wall, 16–17
green, *see* colors

Happiness, 2, 37, 95
harmony, 1, 3, 16, 28, 32, 40,
    42, 53–55, 64, 67, 75
healing, 54–55
health, 28, 48, 52–53, 63–64,
    67
Heaven, 3, 11, 17, 78–82
hills, *see* formations
home, 35, 38, 40–41, 43–44,
    63–75, 84–85, 94
honesty, 39
hot tubs, 73
Hsia Dynasty, 11
huang, 9–10
Huang-ti (*see also* shaman-
    kings), 9

I *Ching,* 6–7, 9, 11–13, 38
illness, 4, 30, 52, 54, 71,
    87–89
imbalance, correcting, 58
intelligence, 34, 38
intuition, 6, 45

King Wen (Duke of Chou), 12
Kwan Yin, 76

Lady of the Nine Heavens, 9
landforms (*see also* forma-
    tions), 7, 17–18, 23–24, 49,
    55, 65
    artificial, *see* Later Heaven
        formations; structures
    natural, *see* Earlier Heaven
        formations
Lao-tzu (*see also* Tao-te-
    Ching), 3
Later Heaven formations, 17,
    78–82
Later Heaven Sequence,
    78–79, 82
leadership, 91
Li Shu, 6
light and reflection, 3–4,
    28–29, 50, 57, 71, 74–75
Lin-shan-i, 11
Lo Shu, 7–8, 11–12
location, *see* site
lo-p'an, 13
love, 41
luck, 2, 23, 48, 52, 65

Management, *see* business function

materials
  glass, 35, 42, 50–51, 57, 61, 71
  iron, 62
  metal, 9, 51, 58–62,
  wood, 9, 36–39, 60–62

Metal, 31–35, 37, 39–44, 58–62, 81, 87
  and Earth, 34, 41
  and Fire, 39, 41
  and Water, 42–43
  and Wood, 37, 41, 44, 60

Ming Dynasty, 47, 82

Ming T'ang, 47

mirrors, 28–29, 75, 79

money, *see* success, financial; wealth

mountain, *see* formations

Nature, 3, 5, 15, 17, 45, 49, 54–55

neighbors, 36, 39–40, 43

nourishment, 33, 36–37, 39, 81, 91

numbers, 7, 11, 45

Office, *see* work place

ornaments, 60–62

Paint, 62

pa-k'ua (see also Eight Tri-grams), 7, 9, 12–13, 31, 78, 89–90

patterns, 17, 24–25, 29, 45–46, 50, 52–53, 74

peaks, *see* shapes

pillar, *see* structures

plants, 44, 59–60, 62, 76

playground, *see* structures

power cables, *see* structures

Primal Beginning (*see also* Taoism), 4

professions
  butcher, 34
  chemical, 34, 38
  commerce, 34–37, 40–41, 43–44, 63, 77, 90
  community service, 40
  construction, 35–36, 50, 63
  creative (*see also* creativity), 2–5, 28, 30, 33, 35, 42, 66, 93
  engineering, 34, 66

professions *continued*
    farming, 34, 36, 55
    financial, 34–35
    information, 34–35, 42, 93
    learning (*see also* public
      buildings, schools), 34,
      38, 41, 54
    manufacturing, 34–35
    mining, 34
    restaurant, 7, 33
profit (*see also* success, finan-
    cial; wealth), 39, 56–57
prosperity, *see* success, finan-
    cial; wealth
protection, 21, 23, 27, 46,
    48–49, 64, 71, 73, 75,
    84–85
Pu Yi, Emperor, 10
public buildings
    hospices, 54
    hospitals, 33, 36, 40,
      54–55
    libraries, 34, 41
    museums, 41
    schools, 36, 40, 45, 55, 96
    police stations, 54
    prisons, 54

Raven, 18–19, 21, 23, 27, 30,
    48–49, 95
recreation, 91
red, *see* colors
relationships (*see also* family),
    48, 53, 73, 79, 81, 89
road, *see* structures
roof, *see* structures
rooms
    basement, 34
    bathroom, 85
    bedroom, 28–29, 50, 64,
      69–70, 72, 84
    corridor, 57, 67–68, 71,
      74–75
    dining room, 74
    foyer, 68
    garage, 34, 57, 70–71
    kitchen, 70–71, 77, 87
    living room, 28, 84
    porch, 56, 73
    study, 28, 72, 88

Schools, *see* public buildings
scientific work, 1, 5–7, 9,
    11–13, 18
sculptures, 59, 62

seasons, 19, 31
  autumn, 19, 31
  spring, 19, 31, 33
  summer, 19, 31
  winter, 19, 31
Seven Portents (*see also* Eight
  Orientations), 82–85, 90, 92
  Accident and Mishap, 82,
    84, 87–88, 93
  Celestial Monad, 82, 84,
    89, 94
  Five Ghosts, 82, 84–86, 92
  Generating Breath, 82, 84,
    88, 93
  Lengthened Years, 82, 84,
    87–88, 93
  Severed Fate, 82, 84,
    86–87, 93
  Six Curses, 82, 84–85, 92
sha, 3–4, 16, 29–30, 46–47,
  49–54, 56–57, 64–76, 79,
  89
  definition of, 29
  deflecting, 75
shadows, 30, 50, 74
shaman-kings, 7, 9
shamans, 6–7, 9, 23

Shang Dynasty, 11–12
shapes
  angles, 18, 29–30, 36, 38,
    47, 61, 75
  arched, 34, 37, 41–42, 44,
    72
  flat, 12, 32, 34, 37, 39–40,
    47, 51, 59–61, 72
  irregular, 35, 37, 60–61,
    64–66
  long, 24, 27, 56, 65,
    68–69, 73–74
  octagonal, 7
  of five elements, 31, 33
  peaks, 24–25, 32, 36, 62
  rectangular, 65
  round, 18, 32–35, 37,
    40–42, 44, 51, 59,
    61–62, 65–66, 72–73
  sharp, 16, 18, 25, 30, 32,
    34, 36, 38, 44, 50–52,
    59, 61–62, 64–66,
    73–76, 93
  slopes, 18, 27, 32–33, 37,
    40, 42, 44, 59, 61–62,
    66, 72
  square, 7, 39, 61

shapes *continued*
  squat, 27
  steep, 16, 24–25, 36, 38,
    52, 54, 66, 69
  straight, 4, 24, 29–30,
    46–47, 49, 69, 76
  symmetrical, 65, 69–70
  tall, 1, 27, 30, 32–33, 36,
    44, 51, 56, 58, 60–62,
    65, 67, 73
  thin, 51, 56, 65
  triangular, 32, 51, 57, 64,
    66, 69, 72
shrine, 85, 92
Shun, Emperor, 10
site, 18–20, 23, 25, 27–30,
  32, 35–44, 46–54, 56,
  58–60, 75, 79, 82, 84
  assessing the Feng Shui of,
    2, 17, 21, 23, 32, 52, 63
  "compound site," 35
  Earth, 37, 39–41, 43
  Fire, 36, 38–41, 43
  Metal, 37, 39–43
  Water, 37, 39, 41–43
  Wood, 36–39, 41–42

smoke, 76
smoothness, 51, 56, 63–65
sound, 75
spring, *see* seasons
stability, 63–64
stairway, *see* structures
statues, 60, 76
stones, 27, 53, 59–60, 76
storage, 28, 34, 85–86, 90,
  92–93
stoves, 70, 74
structures
  balcony, 56
  bridge, 29, 36, 48, 51–53,
    73
  chimney, 32, 62, 65
  column, 30, 32, 36, 60–61,
    66–67, 73
  driveway, 63, 72–73
  fence, 73
  garden, 17, 44, 55, 59, 61,
    73, 75, 94–95
  pillar, 32, 61, 66–67,
    73
  playground, 55
  power cables, 30

road, 16, 30, 52–54, 75, 81
roof, 32, 34, 36–38, 41, 44, 56, 59, 61–62, 66
stairway, 30, 69, 74–75
telephone poles, 30
terrace, 56, 73
walls, 21–22, 61, 65, 68
success, 19, 35–37, 39–41, 56, 72
  commercial, 36
  financial (*see also* wealth), 35, 41
  social and political, 39
summer, *see* seasons

T'*ai chi t'u, see* Primal Beginning; Taoism
T'ai Chi, 28
T'ai Shun, 53
talisman, 7, 79
tall, *see* shapes
Tao, 3
Taoism (*see also yang; yin*), 1, 3–4, 6–7, 31, 77
Tao-te-Ching, 3

telephone poles, *see* structures
terrace, *see* structures
Tiger, 18–21, 23–27, 48–49
  and Dragon, 25–27
Tortoise, 7–8, 18–23, 27, 48–49, 96
traffic, 52–54, 56
trees, 19, 25, 27, 30, 33, 36, 44, 50, 58, 60–61, 73

Unemployment, 65
universal life-energy (*see also chi*), 4

Vertical, 51, 74
violence, 54–55, 65

Walls, *see* structures
Water (*see also* formations), 6–7, 15–16, 18–19, 31–33, 35, 37, 39, 41–48, 50, 53–55, 58–62, 70, 75–76, 81
  and Earth, 41, 43
  and Fire, 39, 43
  and Metal, 42–43
  and Wood, 37, 42

Water Dragon Classic, The, 47

wealth, 19, 28, 34–35, 39, 41–44, 47–48, 53, 57, 66, 71–72

well-being, 37

white, *see* colors

wind, 6–7, 16, 46–47, 76, 81

windows, 28, 30, 50, 57–59, 66, 68, 71

winter, *see* seasons

Wood, 31–34, 36–39, 41–42, 44–45, 58–62, 70, 81

  and Earth. 37, 39

  and Fire, 38

and Metal, 37, 41, 44

and Water, 37, 42

work place (*see also* buildings; business function; professions), 28, 34–35, 37–41, 43–44, 56–58, 72, 84–85, 88, 90–91, 92–96

  best sites for, 35

Yang Yun-sung, 12

yang, 2–4, 15–16, 25, 45, 68, 71, 74, 77–78, 81

yin, 2–4, 15–16, 25, 45, 54, 65, 68, 71, 74, 77–78, 81

Y the Great, Emperor, 10